Public Speaking

Unlock the Secrets to an Emotional and Powerful Presentation, Overcome Fear, and Develop your Confidence, Communication Skills, Social Intelligence, Persuasion Ability, and Charisma

© Copyright 2019

All Rights Reserved. No part of this book may be reproduced in any form without permission in writing from the author. Reviewers may quote brief passages in reviews.

Disclaimer: No part of this publication may be reproduced or transmitted in any form or by any means, mechanical or electronic, including photocopying or recording, or by any information storage and retrieval system, or transmitted by email without permission in writing from the publisher.

While all attempts have been made to verify the information provided in this publication, neither the author nor the publisher assumes any responsibility for errors, omissions or contrary interpretations of the subject matter herein.

This book is for entertainment purposes only. The views expressed are those of the author alone, and should not be taken as expert instruction or commands. The reader is responsible for his or her own actions.

Adherence to all applicable laws and regulations, including international, federal, state and local laws governing professional licensing, business practices, advertising and all other aspects of doing business in the US, Canada, UK or any other jurisdiction is the sole responsibility of the purchaser or reader.

Neither the author nor the publisher assumes any responsibility or liability whatsoever on the behalf of the purchaser or reader of these materials. Any perceived slight of any individual or organization is purely unintentional.

Contents

INTRODUCTION 1

CHAPTER 1: BEING ONE WITH YOUR BREATH 3

CHAPTER 2: PREPPING YOUR MIND, BODY, SOUL, AND VOICE 15

CHAPTER 3: TWO POWER P'S – PACE AND PAUSE 26

CHAPTER 4: HAVE YOU BEEN LISTENING TO YOUR TONE? 34

CHAPTER 5: WHAT'S HAPPENING WITH YOUR HANDS? 43

CHAPTER 6: THE LANGUAGE OF THE EYES 53

CHAPTER 7: GETTING OVER THE STAGE FRIGHT HUMP 63

CHAPTER 8: PUSH WITHOUT BEING PUSHY 74

CHAPTER 9: YOU'RE NEARLY THERE 84

CONCLUSION 95

Introduction

You're standing in front of a room full of people. The spotlight is on you. The crowd is waiting in pin-drop silence to hear what you are about to say. Your heart is pounding. Beats of sweat are starting to form across your forehead. You've never felt so paralyzed with nerves and anxiety —this moment, here, when you are faced with the prospect of public speaking.

Do you think you are the only one who feels this way? Guess again.

Not everyone has natural public speaking skills, but it is something everyone can learn and master by practicing the right techniques. Sure, we would all like to be as confident, charming, and self-assured as some of the most renowned public speakers out there— Tony Robbins, Les Brown, Brian Tracey, or the late Steve Jobs (who is still heralded as among the most remarkable storytellers ever to take the stage.) There's no shortage of famous orators out there who have left an impression on the audiences they have addressed.

But what does it take to become like them? How do they make it look so effortless and natural?

The answer is through a lot of hard work, countless practice sessions, plenty of experience, and having the right techniques up their sleeves. In other words, everything that you are about to discover throughout the next few chapters! Feeling at ease on stage is not an impossible dream if you long for it badly enough and put your mind to it. You will become a powerful, emotional public speaker full of confidence, communication skills, ability to persuade with charisma; audiences are not likely to forget you anytime soon.

There are plenty of books on this subject; we are glad you chose this one. Please enjoy!

Chapter 1: Being One with Your Breath

How does the thought of standing in front of a large - or maybe small - group of people make you feel? Standing before them, preparing to give your speech, knowing that all eyes are on you, watching your every move? Are you nervous, or are you perhaps anxious - feeling like you can't breathe? For a lot of people, public speaking is not something that comes naturally, and difficulty in breathing during a speech is just one of the many factors that they need to contend with.

Shortness of breath or feeling like you do not have enough power behind your voice to project or create enough of an impact does not come down to just nerves alone. Of course, if you are nervous, it is going to make it harder to concentrate on your breathing—but even if you are not someone who's prone to stage fight, you could still struggle with the power of projection. Speakers need to be loud and clear enough that the audience in the back of the room can hear them as if they were standing close by.

If you are struggling with breathing, how do you achieve that? First, you need to pinpoint the reasons behind your shortness of breath. Is it a result of the defense mechanism *fight or flight?* Does It stem from social anxiety? Perhaps you are dealing with *glossophobia* (speech anxiety) – a fear of public speaking. If neither of these scenarios applies and you are someone who's comfortable addressing a crowd, then it could be that you are simply not practicing the right breathing techniques or "being one" with your breath.

Often, nervous speakers who struggle with glossophobia experience the following physical symptoms:
- Accelerated or rapid breathing
- Shortness of breath
- Increased or rapid heartbeat
- Dry mouth sensation
- Tense muscles
- Sweaty palms
- Visibly shaking with nervousness
- Feeling anxious

If you experience any of the following at just the thought of making a public speech, you may be dealing with anxiety over public speaking:
- You become distressed, nervous, and visibly awkward and uncomfortable when you must make a speech
- You become distressed when you feel they that you may be teased or criticized - even the very idea is enough to stress you out
- You become distressed when you find yourself in a situation where you are the center of attention
- You become distressed when you feel you are being watched or observed while you are doing something, i.e., giving a speech
- You become distressed when you have to speak in a formal or public situation - even if just a gathering among friends
- You are easily embarrassed to a point where you start blushing and visibly shaking
- You avoid making eye contact for too long - or not at all

All of these factors (and more) play a role in why you are struggling to breathe when tasked with giving a speech or presentation in any kind of context. Some cases of glossophobia could be so extreme that even if you had to conduct a presentation among friends or fellow colleagues whom you see every day, the very idea of being the only one standing up and having to talk is enough to send you into a tailspin. When you struggle even to compose yourself and keep your heart rate beating at an average pace, it is going to impact your ability to project your voice and deliver and speech with the necessary vigor, power, and enthusiasm that you need to make it useful and effective.

The good news is that this does not have to hold you back forever! Even the most nervous speakers out there can still learn a few tricks of the trade. With copious amounts of practice, these can turn you into the impactful public speaker that you have always wanted to be.

The Power of Your Breath

Let's talk about the power of your breath, as well as how crucial this aspect is for your public speaking performance. Here's an example to illustrate this point:

You're in a meeting room at work, and two of your colleagues are about to present. Colleague A and Colleague B are both talking about exactly the same thing, yet only Colleague B seems to stand out. When the other co-workers who were present at that meeting reflect on it, Colleague B seems to prominently feature in their minds and therefore, gets the credit for the presentation. Even though Colleague A was talking about the exact same thing.

Why does this happen? Because Colleague B was doing something different, and the difference was the way he/she *sounded.* Yes, the way that you sound can be the deciding factor that determines whether you were as effective in your presentation as you should have been. Your audience *knows* the difference between someone who sounds nervous and someone who sounds confident. If you have ever been in the audience when a nervous speaker was presenting, you can tell just how they feel through the subtle tremors in their voice. You may believe you are doing a good job of trying to hide just how nervous you really are, but your body language and the way that you sound will be a dead giveaway, even if you appear somewhat composed on the outside.

Try this quick exercise and say this phrase out loud: *"I have something to say."*

Say that once in a firm and confident voice. Now, say it a second time, but this time try imagining you are nervous or afraid when speaking. Record yourself during this exercise and then play it back. Do you hear the difference? You're saying the exact same thing, yet *the way* you say it has a striking contrast. The clear, strong, and confident voice is going to be the one that resonates with you and stands out the most, and this is just why *Colleague B* was memorable while *Colleague A* was not. Which voice do you want your speakers to hear?

Maintaining the right breathing technique can make a world of difference in how you sound when you are giving a speech or presentation. Singers, for example, are a group of people who understand just how much their voice can be affected by the way that they breathe. Some singers take professional vocal training classes to learn how to breathe better so they can project a loud, strong and powerful voice when they sing so every single audience member can hear them as clear as day. Learning how to *be one with your breath* is the key to turning you into a powerful public speaker, someone who is able to command the attention of the audience from the moment you utter the words, *"Hello, and welcome."*

Yet, despite its importance, breathing techniques are *still* the most overlooked aspect when preparing for a speech. You've prepared yourself mentally, carefully reviewed your material, dressed the part, and practiced your speech a dozen times in your head by now. Yet, *did you prepare with the right breathing exercises to help you project your voice on that day?* Most likely not.

If you want to see just what a difference training your voice and breathing can make, there is a **recording** of former United Kingdom

Prime Minister Margaret Thatcher which illustrates this perfectly. The former Prime Minister undertook voice lessons when she was elected to her post, and the difference in her speech is remarkable. While some speculators believe that she was making a conscious effort to speak in lower tones (there is **research** to suggest that deeper voices have greater success in politics and business), it is, in fact, her *breathing* that is making the most significant difference. With correct breathing techniques, the former UK Prime Minister's voice sounds decidedly richer and more vibrant—and as a result of that, it automatically seems lower, as well.

The Difference Between Shallow Breathing and Deep Breathing

Breathing occurs so naturally to us that we do not even think about it. Unless we make a conscious, mindful attempt to concentrate on the flow of air that moves in and out of our bodies, chances are we could go through the entire day without even giving our breath a second thought. Breathing is the flow of oxygen traveling from our atmosphere into our lungs, involving carbon dioxide movement from our lungs to outside of our bodies. However, little do we realize that there is a lot more to it than the simple inhale and exhale process. There are specific *breathing techniques* involved which differentiate shallow breathing from deep breathing.

Deep Breathing

Deep breathing also referred to as diaphragmatic breathing, which is when we make full use of our diaphragm, purposefully expanding our lungs to their fullest capacity. This can often be seen as our diaphragms press into our abdomen, causing our bellies to expand outwards.

With deep breathing, the expansion is taking place in our abdomen instead of at the chest or thoracic cavity. This technique is considered a focused technique, one which can prove useful as a cure for certain symptoms we may experience. It is technique requiring concentration because it is not something that we naturally do when we breathe at a regular rate. When we're nervous or anxious, for example, we're encouraged to take deep, focused, measured breaths to help us calm our nerves. Deep breathing is also promoted as a temporary relief from headaches, stress, high blood pressure, anxiety, and even pain. Some women use this measured technique to help them through the labor process.

To breathe in deeply, you would need to focus on drawing air in through your nose and consciously thinking about filling your abdomen area with as much air as possible. You would then focus on holding your breath for at least two seconds before you exhale just as deeply in a controlled measure through your mouth. Not only is this technique useful in situations where you need to calm yourself down, but deep, diaphragmatic breathing also lends power and strength to your voice. Among the benefits that come with this breathing technique are:

- It increases the amount of oxygen that your brain receives because you are breathing in more air
- It helps you stay calm by purposefully slowing down your heart rate, forcing you to concentrate on your breathing instead of your nerves
- Taking in excessive oxygen and expanding your abdomen improves your stance, giving you "power pose" instead of the hunched over, nervous posture that you might otherwise project
- Lends clarity and strength to your voice, which in turn gives you an air of authority
- Gives the appearance of confidence

When combined, these benefits give you the authority, credibility, and believability needed to showcase you as a successful public speaker.

Shallow Breathing

Unlike deep breathing, shallow breathing tends to stop at the chest, rather than travel all the way down to the belly and abdomen. Shallow breathing draws only minimal amounts of air into your lungs, moving only the chest area during the breath. Much of the time, this breathing occurs involuntarily, and most people are unaware of this breathing technique. In fact, this is the kind of breathing that we employ every day for our survival; we do not even stop to think about it. As you are reading this right now, consider which type of breathing you are employing. That slow, even pace is your shallow breathing.

Shallow breathing can occur in other instances, like hyperventilation - that even rapid breathing when you are feeling particularly scared, nervous, or anxious. Your breath quickens and gives the appearance of "rapid" breathing because very little air is traveling in and out of your lungs, which causes your breath to quicken. This type of breathing could also be symptomatic of other conditions, including pneumonia, shock, asthma, panic, stress, and other possible health conditions associated with the lungs. The danger with shallow breathing for a prolonged period is that it could quickly lead to carbon dioxide building up in your body, which in turn leads to an increase in the acidity levels in your bloodstream.

If you were to watch a newborn baby's breathing, you'd notice that – instinctively - they often employ the deep breathing technique, providing maximum benefits for their body. Watching them, you'll notice their chest and abdomen rise and fall visibly, an indication that deep breathing is happening. For adults, however, this type of breathing is no longer done instinctively. In general, most people tend to be shallow or thoracic breathers, shifting over time as we grow and acclimatize to the everyday stressors and triggers in our environment.

Shallow breathing is *not beneficial* for your body because it keeps the body in a cyclical stress state. Your stress is causing you to breathe in a shallow manner, *and your shallow breathing,* in turn, is causing you to stress out. Since chronic stress is linked to shallow breathing, getting stuck in a prolonged period with this breathing pattern can have serious consequences on your health. When faced with a public speaking situation, shallow breathing can aggravate your stress levels, causing full-blown panic attacks, dry mouth, difficulty breathing, and even be a precursor for potential cardiovascular problems.

How Proper Breathing Techniques Affect the Sound of Your Voice

The right breathing techniques help you feel calmer and more relaxed, resulting in your voice becoming steadier, stronger, and more compelling. Public speaking is a situation that can challenge you as a person on several levels, yet at the same time, it can be a deeply rewarding, satisfying experience. You only need to observe motivational speakers in action in order to see how true this is. Nothing is more rewarding or exciting than speaking on a subject that you are deeply passionate about - a subject you believe in so much that you want to spread the word and share what you know! The most successful, high-profile, and inspirational speakers in the world have shaped, inspired, and changed the lives of millions with a powerful speech. Leaders have rallied together nations and spurred them to action with the help of a compelling, emotional, and impactful speech.

If you are wondering what the secret is to become a confident speaker, here's the answer: *You are doing it already.* You are *breathing.* Now, you need to learn to be one with your breath and employ the power of deep, diaphragmatic breathing as your most empowering public speaking tool. The phrase, *"Take a deep breath,"* is not just a calming axiom; it is an actual tool that you can use to your advantage when you do it right. Every speaker - motivational or otherwise - that you see on stage moving crowds and leaving a powerful, lasting impression behind *is doing it with the help of deep breathing techniques.*

Regardless of your gender or how powerful your voice is right now, everyone can benefit from certain, specific exercises that you can practice at home and remember to use when you are in front of a crowd.

- **1-2-3-Breathe** - Breathing can be as easy as counting *1-2-3*. Start your deep breathing practice sessions off by mindfully counting *1-2-3* as you slowly and deliberately inhale, and then count *1-2-3* again as you slowly and deliberately exhale. *1-2-3* breathe in, *1-2-3* breathe out. Involve all your senses as you do this. If it helps, combine it with a positive phrase or mantra that helps you feel empowered. As you breathe in and count *1-2-3,* repeat a phrase that helps you stay calm and focused. Do this before a speech, and even during moments of your speech when you may be struggling to feel calm.
- **Stand Tall, Back Straight** - Not to the point you feel uncomfortable but stand straight and tall, so your shoulders are back, and your posture is great. Adopt a stance where your feet are positioned shoulder-width apart, with your weight equally distributed. If you are practicing this at home, raise your arms over your head while you breathe deeply and inhale. As you exhale, slowly lower your arms down to your sides in a controlled manner -do not rush it. Keep your shoulders back the entire time, not hunched. When you are in front of a crowd and giving your speech, the shoulder-width apart and shoulders back stance is the best posture you can adopt. Not only does this allow you to breathe deeply when you need to, standing tall also gives you the appearance of being a confident speaker.

Hand on Belly and Chest - Place one hand on your stomach where your belly button is and take the other hand and place it on your chest. As you breathe deeply, pay close attention to the hand that is moving. When most people breathe, their chest moves up and down; to practice deep breathing, you must keep your chest steady and focus on moving your abdominal area instead. The hand that is on your belly should be the one that makes the most movement now, not the hand on your chest. Practice this at home several times and even several minutes prior to your speech to help you get into a relaxed state of mind.

- **Let Your Breath Support Your Words** - After practicing with a few deep breaths, try speaking, allowing your breath to support the words that come out of your mouth. For this exercise, pick a sentence you would like to try practicing. As you speak, slowly exhale while you do, and let your voice resonate with its full, vibrant, and supported sound. To begin, start by slowly exhaling as you say *1 - 2 - 3 - 4 - 5,* and then do it again except this time, imagine you were giving a speech and say, *"Hello, my name is..."* Slowly exhale while you speak, noticing the difference in the way that your voice sounds when it is accompanied by a deep breath.

Exercises to Improve Vocal Strength

These exercises are designed to help you rely on your abdominal muscles to strengthen the sound of your voice. As you practice these exercises, you want to make sure that you can hear yourself breathing in and out as you do. Aim to do these exercises at least once a day, twice a week, or as often as you feel you need it.

- Start by lying down flat on your back in a comfortable position. You want to be sure that you are comfortable because the next step is putting a book on top of your stomach. If you are not comfortable using a book, placing your hands on top of your stomach works just as well.
- Now, as you breathe in from your mouth, feel the way the book (or your hands) is rising. As you exhale, feel it lower. This step should feel natural and effortless. Practice this for several minutes.
- The second step begins with you sitting upright in a chair. Keep your shoulders back, sit up tall, and place one hand on your stomach.
- Repeat the same breathing motions you did when you were on your back, and this time observe the movement of your hand as you feel your stomach moving in and out with each

breath. It helps to sit in front of a mirror and watch yourself doing this.

- After a couple of practice sessions, try saying "hmmm" as you release your breath through your nose. You want to do this deliberately and "feel" the vibration around your nose as you do. The "hmmm" sound should be resonating from your nose, not your throat.
- Next, move onto saying actual words instead of "hmmm." Start with a short word like "up." To do this right, it has to sound as though you are saying "hup," instead of "up." That's how you know you are doing it right. Once you are comfortable, progress to longer sentences and words, like "Up, one ...up, two... up, three" and continue all the way up to 10. Remember to take a deep breath after each phrase.
- Once you are comfortable with this exercise, move on to longer phrases, like you would with a speech. Say, "I'm going to buy some food," and practice saying it with the breathing techniques you learned above. Remember that the breath should be coming in from your mouth, and the air is released as you speak out loud.

These exercises help you remain conscious of allowing the air to flow from your abdomen for maximum power instead of coming from the thoracic area. As you continue to practice, it begins to feel easier and more natural until eventually, you'll be able to do this effortlessly in any speech or presentation.

Bonus Tip: Don't Forget to Smile!

When you are feeling nervous, sometimes the best thing to do smile through it all. Smiling not only brings people together, but it also makes you appear more approachable, and it triggers emotional changes in the body, too. A good dose of laughter triggers endorphins in your brain, and it is just what you need to help you feel relaxed when you need it most—*right before* your public speaking session. The next time you feel particularly anxious over an upcoming presentation, try laughing – *genuinely* - over a funny thought, joke or memory and see what a difference it makes. Even better, try enlisting the help of a friend or colleague to help lighten the mood.

Chapter 2: Prepping Your Mind, Body, Soul, and Voice

Public speaking: you either love it, hate it, or are completely terrified by the very thought of it. There's certainly no shortage of advice out there, telling you how to overcome and prepare for a presentation despite your fears—but they may only overwhelm you more. Have you heard the old adage about picturing everyone in the audience in their underwear? That's not going to help – not when your mind is racing a mile a minute, wishing you were anywhere else but on stage or in front of a room addressing a crowd. Advice will come and go. Some will work well for you, while others do not help at all. There is only one tried and true approach to public speaking that continues to hold true: *you must prepare mentally, physically, emotionally, and vocally* for what's ahead.

Feeling tense or nervous before a presentation or a speech is normal. Even the best speakers out there occasionally experience moments where they feel butterflies in the pit of their stomach. Being nervous is not uncommon. To combat the nervousness, you must prepare yourself mentally and physically – through exercise. You might hear the term "loosening up" thrown about quite a bit, and that refers to the exercises which help you feel more confident and prepared the stage.

The exercises that you are about to work through right now are ideal for anyone who could use a little help relaxing before their big speech. Whether you are a beginning or seasoned speaker, these exercises are designed to help you maintain the calm and focus that you need to get through your presentation.

Physical Exercises to Loosen Up the Body

Stiff and tense muscles are a hindrance to calmness when you are in front of your audience. When you are not relaxed, your body is going to show, and your listeners will sense your discomfort. Try the following physical exercises to get rid of some of that tension in your muscles:

- **Start at the Neck and Shoulders** - Neck and shoulder roll exercises are great for relieving pressure and tension in the upper body. Especially since the neck and shoulder area is where we typically feel most of the strain. The expression *"feeling like a weight has been lifted off my shoulders"* perfectly illustrates what significant impact stress can have on your body. When you are standing for your speech, these tense muscles can make you feel extremely uncomfortable, making it hard to focus on your points. These exercises are easy enough to do anywhere you are, and you should certainly do these a couple of times prior to your speech. Roll your head from one side to the other, moving it in a slow, deliberate circular fashion. Think of it as drawing a circle in the air, but with your head. Roll your shoulders forward, also in a circular fashion like you are attempting to draw a circle in the air. Do this a couple of times, and then switch and rotate them backward.
- **Stretching Out Your Arms** - Take your shoulder relief one step further by stretching out your arms. We use our arms a lot during a presentation or a speech and having stiff

or painful muscles can hinder your gesturing. This, in turn, could affect the power and delivery of your speech when the proper gestures or hand signals do not accompany the point you make. Stretching your arm muscles before a speech can loosen the strain you feel, and significantly improve your body language when you are not in such discomfort. Stretch out your arms in front of you as far as you can, holding the position for several minutes. It should feel really good when you release that stretch. Repeat this move, stretching them behind you, and to the side, too.

• **Do the Twist** - Not the dance move, but waist stretches instead to relieve the pressure from your torso and lower back area. When you are standing during your speech, the last thing you want is to be distracted by the pain in your lower back or torso area, which might even affect your posture and the way that you stand. Remember, posture and stance are important in delivering a confident persona to your audience. These exercises are also easily performed anywhere on the go. Stand with your feet slightly apart, place your hands on your hips and rotate your waist from side to side, once again attempting to draw a circle in the air with your body. Rotate from left to right, alternating from right to left.

Vocal Exercises to Help You Prepare

Now that your body is relieved from some of that strain, it is time to move on to vocal exercises to help you prepare for your upcoming presentation. Vocal exercises are important to ensure that your anxiety does not translate through your voice. A powerful speaker sounds confident, and your voice needs to be strong and steady enough to command the attention of every single person in that room.

• **Start with the "Shush"** - This is where you begin your deep breathing techniques. Relax your shoulders, pull them back, stand up tall, and place your hands on your belly.

Now, take deep, measured breaths, pushing your stomach in with your hands. Exhaling and pushing out all the air you just took in, say *"SHHHHHHHHHHHHHH,"* as loudly as you can, keeping your shoulders down as you do. If it helps, picture yourself as a librarian or teacher who is shushing your students. This should help further relax your body and prepare you for the next few vocal exercises.

• **Trill the Tongue** - Yes, it is just what it sounds like. You're about to warm up your tongue, too, so it is nice and relaxed when you are ready to give your speech. Trilling the tongue involves a simple maneuver of rolling your tongue as fast as you can in your mouth. What you are basically trying to do is force the air in your mouth to go past your tongue is such a fast manner that your tongue feels like it is vibrating almost. Linguists call this little exercise the "rolling of the R's."

• **The Hum** - Humming is the quickest way to relax your vocal cords and warm them up in preparation for your presentation. The vibrating sensation loosens your vocal cords. Start with a long *hmmmmmmm*, and keep the sound going for as long as possible. Then, try doing it without pressing your lips together, keeping your jaws, cheeks, lips, and mouth nice and relaxed as you do. Finally, try humming in ascending and descending tones, increasing and lowering your voice as you do.

• **Enunciate It** - Your final vocal exercises are going to be pronouncing and articulating your words as clearly as possible. Pronounce each *T* and *P* sound as distinctly as possible. Choose several sentences to practice with, enunciating each word in that sentence, opening your mouth wide so that it seems as though you are speaking in an exaggerated manner - which you are.

• **Do the Tongue Twist** - Instead of twisting your waist this time, you are going to now focus on twisting the tongue instead. Tongue twisters are great to help you practice your speech, avoiding the dreaded mumbling, speaking too quickly or even "swallowing" parts of your sentences or words. Those downfalls will kill your presentation. Your audience *must* understand what you are saying, and tongue twisters offer the ideal solution. These twisters force you to repeat similar sound patterns; saying them out loud during the exercises forces you to focus on what you are saying. If you have ever had to say a tongue twister before, you'll know just how much concentration goes into getting the sentence out just right to avoid your words coming out garbled.

Mental Exercises for Improved Concentration During Your Speech

Our brains are fascinating: they are capable of experiencing many emotions, brainstorming, mentally juggling multiple thoughts and solutions, sourcing memories at any given time, and more. Often, we mistake the human brain and *the mind*, thinking that they are the same thing. Nothing, however, could be further from the truth.

The brain is an organ, functioning much like the rest of our organs do. The mind, on the other hand, is a representation of our emotions and thoughts. Put differently, the brain is the organ which houses our mind. Just how our minds work has been the subject of many areas of study, including psychology, neuroscience, and human philosophy. What makes you tick? What's going on in my head? Why do we come up with the thoughts that we do? One of the ways in which the human mind works is that it is driven by the *information at hand*.

Since our mind is where our emotions take place, the mind is responsible for how we feel *before* and *during* the speeches that we make. To give your best performance at every presentation you make, you need to be in the right frame of mind. A mind that is overrun with emotions of fear, worry, and anxiety cannot concentrate on the task and hand. The ability to stay focused during your speech is going to be the difference between a presentation that was "alright", and one that was "outstanding."

If becoming an outstanding public speaker is where you want to be, then you need to start training your mind with the right mental exercises to help you hold onto those powers of concentration, especially when under intense pressure. Mental warm-ups prepare you for getting into the "zone"; the following exercises will be what you need to help strengthen your focus and concentration.

Before starting, you must find a place that is free of distractions. Find a space that is quiet and comfortable, where you can easily settle into as you start working on your concentration levels. It is very important that you remain comfortable throughout the session; if not, you'll become easily distracted by any discomfort, making it hard for you to get started off on the right foot.

- **Find an Object of Focus** - Once you are in your quiet zone, find an object you can focus on and place it in front of you. Begin focusing only on your object, starting with small intervals of time, ranging between 3 to 5- minutes. Maintain your focus throughout that period, concentrating on nothing except the object in front of you. Once you are able to maintain this prolonged period of concentration without distraction, slowly increase the time increments. Bring it up to 10-minutes, then 15-minutes and so on. Train yourself over time to increase your concentration for longer and longer periods.

- **Creating a To-Do List for Distractions** - It may sound strange, but it works. Our minds are prone to wandering, and you will find odd thoughts crossing your mind when you least expect it. Instead of leaving these random thoughts to their own devices, try writing them down whenever they pop into your head, especially if they are concerns you possess over speaking in public. Throughout the day as you go about your daily routine, when a random thought pops up, make a note of it by writing it down so you can come back to it again at a later time. Write it down and then immediately put that thought out of your mind and return to the task you were doing before that thought interfered. This is also a great exercise that trains you to snap back into your focused mode whenever you are briefly distracted.

- **Being Mindful Throughout the Day** - Instead of going through the motions, try being mindful of everything that you do throughout your daily routine. We do a lot each day without giving much -if any- thought to the task. Remember our breathing? Now that you are working on increasing your mental focus, being mindful throughout the day is a useful exercise to enhance that focus. Be mindful of everything, even simple things like putting on your socks, brushing your teeth, or eating your meals. Being mindful of what you are doing and of your surroundings is going to train you to concentrate on being present and observant. It forces you to pay attention to what is essential.

More Specific Techniques, Exercises, and Warm-Ups – Discreet and Easy

Even the most nervous public speaker can perform certain exercises to help them feel more comfortable before a big speech or presentation. It might not completely get rid of the butterflies in your stomach, but it does help you feel a lot more composed and in control. Besides preparing your material, rehearsing it several times, practicing your breathing, and working on your vocal exercises, your body language is another factor that must be considered. Body language can make a significant impression on your audience, so you'll need to make sure yours is sending the right message!

Your body language is going to tell your audience what they need to know about you as a speaker. Are you convincing? Are you confident? Or are you so nervous that you can't wait to get it over with? Are you rushing through your speech because you want to get off the stage? Your confidence as a public speaker is going to in the way you carry yourself, not just by the words coming out of your mouth.

Exercise #1: Working on Your Power Pose

There is evidence that adopting a power pose stance can actually help you feel stronger and effective. U.S-based social psychologists Dana Carney, Andy Yap, and Amy Cuddy put forth this **theory** in 2011, claiming that power poses help lower cortisol and raise testosterone levels.

In other words, standing in a power pose drops your stress levels and raises your feelings of dominance. Pretending to feel more powerful eventually leads to feelings of confidence. To practice this move, stand tall in front of a mirror with your feet shoulder-width apart and shoulders back, adopting good posture. Rest your hands on your hips (like Superman!) Hold this pose for several minutes until you start to feel more confident. When you are on stage or in front of the room, giving your presentation, imitate the power pose, tilting your body towards different areas in front of you. This forward-tilt towards different areas of the room helps your audience feel connected and included.

Exercise #2: Good Eye Contact

There may be a lot of people in the room, but you still need to try and maintain good eye contact with as many audience members as possible, even when you are feeling nervous. Eye contact with the audience helps foster a connection, making it seem as though you are speaking directly to them. This helps an audience feel valued and important, making it more likely to listen and pay attention during your speech. Think about the speaker who merely reads from his notes and barely glances up at the audience; his listeners will lose interest soon.

Good eye contact also fosters that element of trust, since eye contact avoidance is notoriously linked to lying or being dishonest. Practice good eye contact in your daily interactions. Whenever you find yourself having a conversation with someone, hold the connection for no more than 10 seconds before breaking away quickly and then resuming eye contact. Anything more than ten seconds can be interpreted as intimidating.

When you are addressing a crowd, hold eye contact with one audience member for no more than 4 seconds before you move on to the next person so that it does not seem as though you are focused on just one person alone. Your eye contact during a presentation should take on a "Z" formation. For example, you start by looking at the person sitting in the far-left seat. Then, your eyes should travel to the person on the right, sitting in the same row. Then, move forward to the front left, and then the front right. Picture it like you are drawing the letter "Z" through your audience with your eyes.

Exercise #3: Move and Pace

Standing stiffly and rooted to one spot on the stage is the worst thing you could do as a public speaker. You're not showing strong leadership or confidence when you do that. You may be an expert on your subject, but you are not going to convince anyone unless your body language shows it. Moving around the stage shows confidence, and it gives the impression that you are speaking to everyone in the audience. Taking charge and owning the space around you is something a strong leader does. That is the signal you want to send your audience.

When practicing your speech at home, imagine you are in front of your audience, working on your timing and pacing. Avoid moving and pacing too much, though, because that is going to be distracting. Ideally, you should wait for 3-minutes before moving from one area to the other. Practice this at home in front of a mirror if possible, so that in your real performance, your movements seem effortless and natural. Another element is *timing your movements* so that your movements are in sync with subject changes. Each time you ask your audience a question, or creating emphasis on a point, move forward towards the crowd.

When using a mirror in practice, be sure you can always see yourself when you move around. Likewise, on speech day, your audience should always be within your line of vision. Avoid turning away or having your back turned to any part of the audience—this leads to feelings of disconnection. When you talk to someone in person, you will not turn your back on them; aside from being rude, it makes them feel excluded and unimportant. That's the same approach you want to use when you are addressing any crowd.

Exercise #4: Facial Expressions

While your audience may be observing your body language, they will also be closely watching your facial expressions, assessing whether you are genuine or not. Listeners respond better to a speaker who is expressive, whose face tells the story in a powerful way. This exercise, once again, works best in front of a mirror where you can see what you are doing. Observe the facial expressions you make as you rehearse your speech. Does your expression match the message you are trying to convey?

Exercise #5: Observing Your Mannerisms

Sometimes we do not see or know our own mannerisms until someone else points them out. Mannerisms are the habits that rise to the surface when we're nervous, and these can be distracting, causing your listeners discomfort. That discomfort, in turn, may keep them distracted and unable to focus on your message. Fiddling and fidgeting, for example, are nervous mannerisms. Others include excessive gestures, putting your hands in your pockets, crossing your arms in front of your chest, and even using too many filler words like "umm."

To overcome this, record yourself when practicing at home, playing it back, and carefully watching your own performance. Have a friend or family member watch it with you so they can give you their feedback on what mannerisms they think you need to discard. Make a list of your mannerisms, and work on dumping them as you continue with several more practice runs of your speech. Record yourself each time to see if there is any improvement.

Chapter 3: Two Power P's – Pace and Pause

In order to deliver a presentation that is going to leave an impact long after you are finished, it is not enough to just stand in front of your audience and deliver the material you have prepared. Facts, numbers, and interesting revelations are good—but there is still more that needs to be done if you want your crowd to keep talking about your speech long after it is over.

For an effective presentation, you'll need to incorporate the *6-P System* as part of your design and delivery:

- ***Preparation*** *(Before)* - The very first *P* of your process is preparation, which takes place *before* the speech. In this section, you need to think about who your audience is, what you are going to be talking about, how this information addresses their concerns, and how it is going to affect or benefit them. Which of your main talking points do you want them to recall the most?
- ***Planning*** *(Before)* - After the *Preparation,* next comes the planning. Here, the questions to be addressed are what your introduction and conclusion should be, and how you intend to structure your presentation. How do you include all the

most vital information in the most concise manner? How much visual reinforcement should you include in your presentation? How long should your presentation last? How many slides should you include in your PowerPoint, if you are using one?

- ***Practice** (Before)* - Practice as many times as you can before your presentation. Practice at home, in your car, and any time you have a free moment to spare. Practice in front of your family, your friends, even in front of a camera. Watch recordings of yourself, seek feedback from family and friends, and look for areas of improvement you can tweak.

- ***Project** (During)* - For your speech to be effective, you need to remember the next *"P"* in the process, which is to *project* your voice as much as possible. You need to be loud enough to be heard, but not *too loud* that you sound like you are yelling. This is where the breathing techniques come in play, and you must practice enough for deep breathing to become second nature.

- ***Pace** (During)* - To allow your message to resonate and sink in with your audience, you need to pace yourself during your speech. Incorporating difference paces during your speech helps to alleviate monotony and boredom. During the exciting, interesting parts of your speech, speeding it up a little can create a sense of excitement and anticipation in your audience, keeping them on the alert for what's coming next. Slowing the rate of your pace at certain points in your speech helps to build a sense of importance surrounding your information.

- ***Pause** (During)* - Closely linked with pace, these last two *P's* work in tandem to create a maximum impact during your presentation. Pausing during the parts of your presentation (i.e., when delivering your most important information) gives emphasis to your points. This provides your listeners with the needed time to allow the information to sink in before you move onto your next key point. Some of the best speakers out there are at the top of their game because they know just how to pace their speech while skillfully utilizing pauses to make the most out of their delivery.

Out of the *6-P's* listed above, pay the closest attention to the final two.

Using Pace and Pause to Your Advantage

Knowing when to pace and pause during your speech - and using them to your advantage to emphasize certain points - will guarantee that your speech will be exciting and enticing. When you keep your audience guessing, they will be intrigued, hanging onto your every word without even trying. Without the power of *pace and pause,* you could have the most riveting subject in the world, but that won't be enough to stifle those yawns or stop your listeners from zoning out.

The Drawbacks of Being a Fast Talker

For your audience to sit up and pay attention, you need to be the one who sets the pace. You're the commander of the room now, and it is up to you to execute the perfect delivery. Many new or inexperienced public speakers often struggle at the beginning with poor control over their pace, mostly because they are nervous, and it shows. Many new speakers often talk too fast, not pausing enough during their speech, which only makes them sound even *more nervous* than they already are. It's hard for your audience to pay attention when they are not given enough time to process what you are saying. How can they, when you are rushing through your speech from one point to the next?

When you rush, it is clear that you have no control over your emotions and that your nerves are getting the best of you. And yes, your audience will see this clearly, as well. Talking too fast forces your audience to work even harder to try and understand what you are saying. Bear in mind: your listeners have come with the expectation of *not having to work hard to listen.* To them, you are the one doing all the work as the presenter. Their job is just to sit there and listen – and they expect it to be an easy job! As soon as they have to exert themselves trying to absorb what you are saying, it won't be long before they tune you out; it is just too much work.

The beauty of speech is about connecting with others. You've been given an opportunity to connect with a group of people all at once, but that becomes hard to do when they can't understand you.

There are other negatives from failing to pace yourself during your speech:

- Your audience assumes that you are nervous and lack confidence, hurrying as much as possible to finish and get off the stage.
- You will lack clarity and volume, since talking too quickly won't allow you to take in the necessary air that you need to help your voice project loud and clear.
- Your diction becomes compromised. Talking too fast does not give your tongue enough time to keep up with your mind, and as a result, important consonants and vowels can be lost. When this happens, the essence of your message is no longer well-received by your audience.
- Fast-talking causes confusion when your audience can't keep up. Remember that you may understand what you are saying, but that does not mean that they do. Trying to win over your audience is going to be much harder to do when they find your speech confusing.
- You run the risk of having your audience view you negatively. Your credibility is at risk when you appear impatient, perhaps even aggressive. Additionally, talking fast shows that you lack empathy for your listener, failing to take their feelings into consideration. Not every listener processes information the same way, and some might need a bit more time than others. Talking too fast shows you have little regard for their needs, that you are only thinking about yourself and getting your speech over with.

As a speaker, learning to pace yourself is going to be one of your greatest assets. True, you may be nervous and probably can't wait to get off the stage and retreat out of the spotlight, but you shouldn't let your audience know that. Pace and pause are masterful public speaking techniques that only a handful of great speakers have managed to accomplish. You can learn to hone these skills, too.

Learning to pause during a speech affords several benefits, yet it continues to remain one of the most overlooked public speaking techniques. This is likely because nerves often win out at the end of the day. When emotions run high, it is hard to concentrate on anything else. Here's what happens when you learn to pause during your speeches effectively:

- Researcher Brigitte Zellner notes in her **research** that pausing helps your audience better understand you and that the communication process becomes a lot more intelligible as a result. Zellner references even further research by Grosjean and Deschamps (1975), which points out that complex communicative tasks require more pausing. According to Zellner, when pauses occur during communication, a great deal of improvement can be seen in terms of speech comprehension. In other words, since your audience is not going to have the benefit of reading bullet points, bold, italics or punctuation, it is up to you to "create this" in your speech through your pauses and paces.
- Pauses allow your speech to sound more polished, cohesive, coherent, and professional—instead of filling up that time with filler words of no value. It also gives you time, as the speaker, to think about your next talking points, and allows your mind to catch up with your mouth.
- Further **research** indicates that pauses can effectively convey emotions, especially when the pauses are well-timed. Depending on what you say, your pauses are going to vary based on whether you are trying to convey happiness, enthusiasm, frustration, or any other kind of emotion. For

pauses to be used authentically, you need to imagine you are speaking to your audience the way that you would with a family member or a friend.

- If you need help controlling the overall pace of your delivery, pauses are the way to do it. Your audience can only absorb information at a certain rate, and when you pace yourself and pause, you are allowing your rate to match the listening capabilities of the majority of your audience. **Research** shows that during a speech, three types of pauses tend to occur. Brief pauses (1/4 of a second), medium pauses (up to one second) and long pause of over one second's duration. Short

Pausing allows you to conduct the deep breathing techniques you need to take in more air, which allows your voice to adjust and be ready to project in a steady, clear manner once you start speaking again.

- Pauses allow time for reflection, and when your audience is given a chance to mull over what you have told them, this increases their engagement rates during the question and answer portion of the presentation.

The following techniques are meant to help you nail the right pace and know when to pause for effect so that your speech packs the powerful punch that you hoped for. Do it right, and your pauses during your speech will seem so effortless—and your audience won't be consciously aware of it.

- **Don't Memorize Your Content** - The likelihood of you rushing through your speech is greater when you memorize your facts. The key is to *understand* your subject and know your material so well that you do not need to memorize your content word-for-word.
- **Break It into Chunks.** Take a look at your speech and see where you can break it off into smaller sections or chunks. Reading your speech aloud a few times will help you observe

which sections you could plan for your pauses to make it sound more natural.
- **Practice with A Metronome** - There's a useful app for just about anything these days, including practicing your speech. Metronomes can be great tools that help you practice your pace, allowing you to adjust your tempo accordingly as you begin to get a better feel of how fast or how slow you are speaking.
- **Stretching Out Your Vowels** - Non-English speakers use this technique to help them slow down and remain focused on what they say. For this exercise to work, you need to take your time pronouncing your vowels as clearly as possible (but not too slow to the point where you begin to sound unnatural).
- **Fight the Urge to Rush** - When you are nervous, there is going to be a little voice in your head that keeps telling you to "*hurry up!*" so you can get out of there as soon as possible. You're going to have to work very hard to tune that voice out. You worked hard on your presentation, and you know you have got some great material and fantastic benefits for your listeners. You should give them the opportunity to absorb the essence of your message fully and fighting the urge to rush is how you do it. Slow down, take a step back, breathe, count to five, and then resume.

How Do I Tell If I'm Speaking Too Quickly?

To you, your speech rate might be just perfect, but that is because you are so used to the way that you speak, you do not see anything wrong with it. Ask a stranger, however, and they might have a completely different view of the way that you talk. In your mind, you might believe that you are adopting the perfect pace, but to your listener, you could be outdistancing their ability to keep up.

Determining your speech rate (the speed at which you speak) is a very useful piece of information. This speed is calculated based on the number of words that are spoken in a minute. General speed rate guidelines dictate the following classifications of speech rates:

- **Slow speech rate:** *Less than 110 Words-per-Minute (WPM)*
- **Conversational speech rate:** Somewhere between *120 WPM to 150 WPM*
- **Fast speech rate:** *Exceeds 160 WPM*

Examples of a conversational speech rate are podcasters and radio hosts, who, on average, speak anywhere from 150-160 WPM. In case you need an example of how to sound natural or conversational during a speech, it might be helpful to listen to several podcasts beforehand. You might also find it helpful to watch several videos on speeches by Barack Obama, Amy Tan, or Steve Jobs – all exemplary role models of well-paced public speakers.

An example of how you *do not* want to speak during a presentation is like an auctioneer or a commentator. On average, they utter anywhere from 250-400 WPM, which is much too fast and completely inappropriate for an effective presentation.

Chapter 4: Have You Been Listening to Your Tone?

Speeches—they can either be great or terrible. Even the most well-put-together presentations (or even ones at a mediocre level) can end up being terrible on the actual day of the presentation. When that happens, there is usually one reason for it—*it is uninspiring and boring.* You could have done everything right up to that point. You prepared. You practiced. You even did your breathing exercises and vocal warm-ups. Yet, the presentation was uninspiring and dull because it wasn't delivered in an interesting manner. That alone makes a difference, and you either end up with a room full of attentive, alert and engaged listeners—or a room full of sleepy, zoned-out listeners who are idly checking their phones and counting the minutes until your speech is over.

How Using Varied Vocal Tones Can Make a Difference

Monotonous speakers tend to be the dullest and most uninspiring kind; nobody wants to sit and listen for half an hour or more to someone who speaks with little to no variation in their tone of voice. Varying your vocal tone not only engages your audience, but it also energizes your words through the emotional inflections used in your speaking. Before this can happen, *you* need to be emotionally invested and interested in what you are talking about. If you are not passionate about your topic, then you are not the right person to speak in public about that subject. Motivational speakers like Les Brown and Tony Robbins can move audiences and strike an emotional chord with them *because* they believe in what they preach. They're passionate about their topics, and this passion shines through every word of every sentence that they speak.

Giving a speech does not mean you should sound stiff and rigid. In fact, you should *let* your audience witness the full range of emotions that you feel when you talk about certain aspects of your speech. When the statistics leave you feeling angry or frustrated, let them know it. When you are excited about a new revelation, show them how you feel and allow them to share in the excitement, too. Be animated from the moment you walk onto the stage and use your emotional inflections to help you tell a story with your speech.

Go back and review Chapter 1. In the example of Colleague A and Colleague B, one was more memorable than the other even though they were presenting on the same subject. The difference was due to the *way* each colleague presented their points. You could be saying all the right things, but if you do not say it in the right *way,* it is not going to be effective!

The Way You Say It Matters

Consider this scenario: You've noticed your work buddy with a miserable, grumpy, and unhappy expression on his face. He's frowning, his arms are folded across his chest, and everything about his body language is screaming out loud for you to back off. Yet, you do what any concerned colleague would do, venturing to ask him if he's okay. He responds, "I'm fine," but his smile is forced, and his tone is clipped. From the way he responds, you instinctively know that everything is *not fine,* despite what he is saying. It clear that his body language does not match his message.

It does not matter what words are coming out of your mouth—it is your *tone of voice* that determines how well your message is received by your audience. The inflection of your voice, the volume at which you speak, your pace, and your tone are all the elements that come together and contribute to the effectiveness of your speech. Dr. Albert Mehrabian, a professor and psychologist renowned for his work and publications on verbal and nonverbal communication and its relative importance, understood what a significant role our voices play in our speech.

Dr. Mehrabian created what is now known as the *7-38-55 Rule for Personal Communication*. Using this formula, a communication that is going to be 100% successful is going to come down to how well you follow the formula. In this rule, 7% of communication comes from your words, while 38% is the way that you convey these words, and the remaining 55% is the body language that is used when delivering your message. The fact that 38% belongs to the way we say things is a big indicator of just how important tone of voice is in the communication process.

The tone of voice boils down to attitude. Your voice is not going to change. It's the way that you *speak* that is going to alter the effectiveness of your speech. Give a presentation when you have had a particularly rough day, and in a bad mood, then your speech won't be nearly as impactful; your heart is not in it. When your heart's not in it, your tone will be the dead giveaway. Forced passion and cheerfulness will never sound as convincing as the real deal. If you haven't been having much luck with your speeches so far, this might be one reason why!

Monotony is Boredom

Monotonous or unvaried speech is not just boring to listen to, but it also makes a speaker sound disinterested in their own presentation. Your audience might also assume that you are not confident about your own thoughts or ideas, and that is why you sound as if you were doing nothing more than reading from a script. Monotony has no compassion, no emotion, and no feeling behind it—which is why it does very little to inspire your audience, making for a terrible speech presentation. No audience member wants to sit through all of that and walk away feeling like they got nothing beneficial out of the session.

Monotonous speech delivery is an all-too-common pitfall for many speakers – and one that can easily be avoided. It's not just new speakers that fall prey, seasoned speakers still struggle with shaking off old habits. Nothing kills communication like a monotone voice, and you will lose your audience within the first five minutes of the speech if you do not learn to liven up your speaking voice.

It is *impossible* for your audience to maintain an interest in what you are saying if you are boring. You've probably had to sit through a few less-than-thrilling presentations in your lifetime, so you'll understand just how hard it can be. Struggling to maintain focus when the speaker is doing nothing to encourage the situation can only result in one thing: you tune them out quickly. As the speaker, once again, your message has failed to make the impact that you hoped it would, and you can't quite figure out why.

Here's a couple of other problems that monotone delivery presents:

- Your audience perceives you as dull and uninteresting when you sound like you are droning on and on about a bunch of memorized facts.
- Monotone voices are often perceived to be shifty and untrustworthy because there is no emotion behind the message.
- Your audience does not see you as upbeat or cheerful, and if you are presenting on a subject with good news in it, your voice is going to contradict the message that you are trying to send.
- There are inconsistencies between what you say and your body language, which makes you appear untrustworthy or shady.

Thankfully, it is not the end of the world if you do happen to struggle with monotony and a lack of variety in your vocal tones when presenting. The exercises listed below are designed to help you get more out of your vocals, so you will be saying the following sentences differently each time.

Exercise #1

Say the following sentence, imagining that you are completely ecstatic and giddy with happiness:

"I'm going on vacation in two days."

Now, repeat the sentence above, but this time imagining that you were extremely unhappy, miserable, and sad. Observe the difference in the way that you sound. Practice with several sentences and alter the emotions you feel when you utter these sentences out loud. Practice with sentences while imagining that you feel impatient, angry, professional, business-like, disinterested, fatigued, and any other emotion you can think of. Imagine the emotion, then say the sentence out loud while pouring as much emotion into your delivery as you can.

Exercise #2

Pick a passage from a book, magazine, newspaper, or any online content. Each day spend at least 15-30 minutes (or any amount of spare time you have) reading these passages aloud.

As you do, once again imagine reading the sentence as though you were actually going through the emotions that the writer conveys. Include some facial expressions with your delivery if it helps. Don't hold back - you are practicing on your own with no one to impress. Be as over the top or as dramatic as you wish in your reading. The point is to pack as much feeling into what you are saying as possible, varying the tone of your voice.

A good tip would be to record yourself during these sessions, playing it back and see how you sound. Can you tell the emotions that you are supposed to feel based on the way you sound? If you can clearly distinguish one emotion from the next, you are doing a good job.

Exercise #3

This one works best if you have children at home, as you'll have plenty of access to children's books. Children's books are among the best practice material for vocal variation available. When you read aloud to a child, you tend to put a lot of variety into it, mixing up your voices based on the different characters in the book, and exaggerating your facial expressions for the entertainment of the child.

If you do have kids at home, go ahead, and use the time you spend reading to them as a way of practicing your vocal exercises. And if you do not have kids at home, you can still practice anyway with plenty of online resources that give you access to children's content through a quick Google search.

Banish the Monotony Once and for All

There are several benefits to be gained by getting rid of the monotony in your delivery, aside from the fact that your speeches and presentations improve by a mile. As your vocal variety improves:

- Your audience appreciates and respects you more as a speaker because they can see you are putting your heart into it.
- You become more interesting as a speaker, and your audience automatically becomes more interested in you.
- Your audience's interest is piqued, making them more receptive to the points that you are trying to make.

And of course, you are no longer seen as just any boring, forgetful speaker.

How Pitch Conveys Different Emotions and Messages

The ability to communicate well with the people around you is one of the most important life skills you can develop. Successful communication requires that you get your message across clearly and without a doubt. A great resource for emotionally powerful speeches is TED Talks, and one example of such a powerful performance is by speaker Hugh Herr. His speeches are a beautiful example of just how much emotions can go in terms of transcending the delivered content. THAT is the key to giving a great speech, captivating and engaging your audience right from the beginning.

Commonly referred to as "the art of persuasion," it takes great skill to convince others to see things the way that you want them to. When speaking, the goal is not to force others to accept your ideas, the goal is to use your skills to persuade and convince them to agree. To effectively do this, you need to tap into their emotions. It is often the way that you make someone *feel* that leaves the strongest impression. They may forget what you have said, but they will never forget the way you made them feel. If you have ever had fantastic customer experience where the staff member went above and beyond to make you feel valued, you'll know just how valuable a great experience can be. You can't recall just what the staff member might have said, but you do know they made you feel great, and the experience was top-notch from start to finish. You tell everyone that you meet what a great experience you had, too.

The right *emotional* delivery of your speech can recreate the same situation. Even if your audience can't recall word for word what you said during your presentation, they will still go out and spread the word to everyone they know about what a fantastic time they had. To create that memorable emotional encounter for your audience, you need to rely on using the right pitch to do it. Most public speakers tend just to do the easy thing and deliver the content they are supposed to. But that content will never reach the audience on an emotional level if your tone is not combined with the right pitch. These two elements must work together to formulate the perfect delivery.

Your pitch, which is the high and low notes that you hit when you are speaking, should sound natural and pleasant. If your voice is far too high-pitched, you run the risk of being perceived as annoying or far too "squeaky" to your audience. That's not a sound they want to listen to for long! Having a pitch that is too low is not such a good thing either. Lower pitches are often associated with a sense of authority; you may come off sounding too bossy or commandeering – not something which is going to be well-received.

Many people do not realize that they aren't varying their vocal tone when speaking. Again, recording yourself is a great way to tell whether enough variation is taking place when you are speaking naturally. When listening, do you like the sound of your own voice? Chances are if you do not, your audience might not like it either; something needs to change if you are going to become the great public speaker that you want to be. That "something" is your pitch.

Creating the perfect emotional, pleasant experience for your audience means strengthening your message by varying to pitch of your voice based on what you are saying. When you ask a question, for example, end it with a higher pitch sound. When you make a statement, emphasize your point using lower pitches and tones.

Practicing Your Pitch Variety in Your Delivery

Before you begin any of these exercises, it is important that you record yourself during your practice sessions. Before you can begin refining your vocals for better public speaking sessions, you need first to *realize how you sound* to your audience. Recording yourself is the most accurate method of assessing your current vocal abilities, where your strengths and weaknesses lie. The way that you hear yourself is *not the same way others hear you.* Your voice is traveling through the bones in your head, and when that sound finally arrives at your ears, it sounds different to you than to others. This is why how *we think we sound* is not actually how we sound to others.

An Exercise in Pitch

The best way to practice varying your pitch is through several read-aloud sessions. Just like exercises above to vary your tone, once again, you want to pick out several passages to read aloud, but this time, you are going to focus on reading these sentences with a different pitch.

Exercise #1

Pick one pitch to start with. It can be either high or low—it is up to you. Now, read your chosen passage aloud, maintaining the same pitch throughout until you reach the end. If you are starting off with the higher pitch, be sure to keep it high-pitched all throughout your reading. Once you are finished, switch your pitch! If you started with a higher pitch, you'd now be reading that same passage using the lower pitch instead.

Observe the effect that it has on you and how you feel when you use a higher and lower pitch. You should feel both an emotional and a physical difference.

Exercise #2

Once again, pick a passage. This time switch back and forth between your high and low pitch as you read aloud. Imagine your voice on a seesaw, alternating back and forth between the two pitches. You could start by reading the first sentence aloud in a high-pitched voice, and then switch to the lower pitch when you come to the second sentence. In the third sentence, switch to high pitch again, and back to low-pitched on the fourth sentence. Keep this going until you reach the end of your passage.

Once you have got comfortable with this, increase the difficulty level by switching pitches after every three words instead of between sentences. Read the first three words in a high-pitched voice, and then read the next three words using your lower tones. You can vary your pitch alterations as you like and play around with it.

Chapter 5: What's Happening with Your Hands?

Not everyone is going to feel comfortable standing in front of a crowd when they know several pairs of eyes are watching their every move. Being under the spotlight can make it hard to concentrate on what you should say, let alone remembering your breathing and body language at the same time. As if that is not enough, now you need to concentrate on what your hands are doing during your presentation! Yes, the hand signals you are unconsciously demonstrating could be sending out all the wrong signals without you even realizing it, yet it is another common mistake for new public speakers.

Your Gestures Matter

Remember how body language is 55% of the overall communication process? That includes your hand gestures, the subtle cues and signals that you give your audience - often without giving it too much thought. When was the last time you paid attention to what your hands were doing when you were speaking to someone – not while presenting or giving a speech, but just in everyday conversation with a friend or colleague? Do you think about what your hands are saying? Probably not, but the story that your hands tell could unwittingly be contributing to your message in a good (or bad) way.

Your Hand Signals Are Surprisingly Powerful

Research conducted on TED Talks revealed, not surprisingly, that the most popular and well-liked speakers were the ones who used twice as many hand gestures during their presentation. It wasn't just their fluctuating vocal tones and voice pitches that had audiences captivated—it was the various hand signals that they used to keep audiences tuned into the points they were making.

Nervous speakers who are uncomfortable being in front of a crowd need to rehearse their speeches with the accompanying hand gestures well beforehand. It's not going to work if you decide to "wing it" on that day. These influential speakers are so good at what they do *because* they've had plenty of experience and numerous practice hours clocked in before they reached their current level of competence.

Here's why the right-hand gestures can either make or break your message:

- With the right-hand gestures, you present yourself as a confident, composed public speaker who commands the room. Audiences respect that.
- Hand gestures can act as visual cues for your audience, helping to strengthen and further emphasize your points.
- Hand gestures are can be likened to those of an orchestra maestro. Your speech is the musical masterpiece that you are presenting while your gestures are the movements that tie it all together. Combined, they help audiences better focus on and appreciate what's being presented.
- Proper hand gesturing conveys that you are enthusiastic and passionate about what you are presenting (as opposed to standing on the stage stiff and barely making any

movements). When we're excited, we naturally become more animated, and we gesture to emphasize that excitement. The same thing happens during a presentation.

- Your hands can help you better explain a point that you are trying to make. When you are trying to emphasize that the results of a study's findings are "smaller" than expected, using the accompanying hand gestures will help cement this fact into your audience's mind.
- Hand gestures make you appear more trustworthy. Inherently, humans are visual creatures, and we do not rely on words alone to be convinced by what someone is telling us. Which speaker would you trust the most? A speaker who gestures for emphasis or a speaker who has their hands in their pockets or stiffly by their sides the entire time?
- Your hand gestures mimic the thoughts that are going through your mind. Your words may sound confident and assured, but if your hand gestures do not match up to it, your audience will spot that immediately.

If you were to observe some of the most influential, memorable speakers and the way that they present themselves when addressing crowds, you'd notice that hand gestures are used to strengthen certain key aspects of their message. These influential speakers use *more* hand gestures than the average speakers do, and the gestures that they use are well-timed and crowd sensitive.

They know that the audience is paying attention to everything that they do, and they purposely use their body language for stressing particular points the *want the crowd to remember* most.

Using Correct Hand Gestures

Here's a fun fact about hand gestures: we were *all born to do it*! Researchers found that 18-month old toddlers who relied more on hand gestures to communicate went on to have greater language abilities as they got older. Hand gestures are a natural part of who we are as human beings.

Hand gestures are like a second language. Play a game of Charades, and it is obvious that our hands are tools capable of telling a story even in the absence of words. That does not mean, however, that you should gesture any which way you want when you are giving your presentation. No, the most effective public speakers are the ones who rely on a select, chosen few gestures that they learn to execute perfectly. Nervous public speakers suddenly become all too aware of their hands when they are in front of a crowd. Suddenly, hand gestures that normally flow when they are conversing with familiar people seem to disappear! When you are nervous, you forget what to do with your hands altogether, which explains why many new speakers stand stiffly in front of a crowd, looking awkward and extremely uncomfortable.

Sometimes new speakers swing to the other side, gesturing *far too much*, distracting their audience from the core message. Nervous speakers do not realize that they are hands are giving away how anxious they feel. Some examples of what nervous gesturing looks like include:

- "Wind-milling" hands, waving them all over the place
- Constantly pushing glasses back up onto the nose
- Playing with hair
- Clenching and unclenching the fists
- Wringing the hands
- Arms crossed in front of the body, tightly gripping the elbow of the opposite arm
- Thumping a podium or table too often to stress on a point
- Rubbing or scratching the nose too much
- Excessive finger-pointing directed towards the audience

To become an effective public speaker, you must become more aware of what your hands are doing. They need to enhance - not detract - from the message you are sending your audience. Unfortunately, most speakers won't be aware that their gesturing needs work unless someone points it out to them. A few simple rules to keep in mind when it comes to hand gestures are:

- Your hand gesture should clarify or supplement your points
- Your hand gestures should be natural, not obsessive
- Your hand gestures should be used mindfully and with intention
- Consider periodically clasping your hands together to prevent excessive gesturing
- Your palms should be displayed in an open manner, signaling honesty

Certain Hand Gestures Can Be Used to Make Your Speech More Effective and Engaging

If you want people to listen to you, you need to gesture with your hands. **Studies** have discovered that gestures make audiences take notice of your speech's acoustics. As these studies have revealed, hand gestures are not mere "add-ons" but exist for a specific purpose. Yes, hand gestures can be very powerful elements that contribute to your public speaking success. If you have ever been given advice along the way that tells you *not to use your hands too when giving a speech, toss* that advice out the window! The absence of gestures is not the answer to an effective speech. Hand gestures are still a necessity, but the key is to let the correct hand gestures do some of the talking.

The same TED Talks **research** mentioned above also discovered that the speeches which were the least popular were the ones that had an average of only 272 hand gestures incorporated into the presentation. The most popular ones (averaging 7.4 million viewers) had 465 hand gestures included in the speech that ran for the same amount of time as the least popular speeches. A typical struggle-point for speakers is deciding *what the correct hand gestures are* to help reinforce their messages - doing this while also remembering their speaking points. There's a lot that goes into trying to make a speech effective!

Hence, which hand gestures are considered effective and which are nothing more than a mere distraction? What should you use during your presentations to add power to your points? When in doubt, it is best to start with the following gestures:

- **Descriptive Gestures** - These gestures need to be pre-planned when you are practicing your speech. You may be tempted to gesture naturally on that day, but the danger with that approach us you could risk going overboard. Pre-planned, descriptive hand gestures can be a big help in your speeches. Descriptive gestures are used to help the audience stay in sync with what you are saying. If you are trying to make a small point, pinch or bring your fingers as close together as possible. If you are trying to illustrate a big point, expand your arms outwards to highlight what you are saying. When you are talking about numbers that range between one to 10, go ahead and show those numbers with your hands. These descriptive gestures help to paint a visual picture of your points within you audience's mind, helping them better remember your speech.
- **Open Your Palms** - Keeping your palms open is a common piece of advice related to body language. Subconsciously, people associate the open palm gesture as a sign that you have nothing to hide. When criminals are arrested, they are instructed to come out with their hands up as proof they have nothing to hide. Keeping your palms open and displayed to the audience encourages that element of trust because subliminally you are telling them you are exposed and there is nothing dishonest about your intentions.
- **Gesture Within the "Strike Zone"** - The "Strike Zone" is the area which spanning from your shoulders to the upper portion of your hips. Within this range is where your hand gestures appear the most natural, and ideally, you want to keep your gestures within this zone. Anything more than this and you risk gesturing in a distracting manner, rather than the effective one you are aiming for. Although it is not a hard and fast rule, it does err on the side of caution. It's okay if you need to gesture outside this zone occasionally.

- **The "Hand Over Heart" Gesture** - This is a good gesture to use when you are trying to emphasize that a certain point is particularly important to you. For example, when you are telling your audience during your speech that *"this cause is so important/matters a lot to me,"* placing your hand over your heart as the accompanying gesture adds that emotional element to your words.
- **The Double Hand Gesture** - Use this only when you need to use your hands to represent two groups or two important points that you want to draw the audience's attention to. Using both hands to gesture as you speak is useful when you are comparing two opposing points. This makes it easier for your audience to keep track of the two points that you are referring to. When you talk about Point A, for example, raise your left hand to remind your audience that Point A is what they should be focusing on right now. When you talk about Point B, raise your right hand and lower the left. This reminds the crowd that a different point of view is being addressed now, and their focus should now be shifted to Point B. The double hand gesture is useful in situations where you need to help your audience keep track of what's going on so that they aren't left behind each time you switch tracks.

Hand Gesturing Mistakes to Avoid

It was briefly touched on above what some examples of nervous hand gesturing look like. Remember the mannerisms we discussed in Chapter Two? Hand gestures fall into this category of nervous mannerisms that come out when you find yourself in a less than comfortable situation (like being in the spotlight and having to make a speech in front of everyone!) Playing with your hair, fiddling with objects in your hand, tugging at your clothes, picking at your nails, putting your hands in your pockets, flailing your arms in an uncoordinated manner are all examples of what *not to do* when you are giving a speech.

If in doubt and you are *still* not sure what to do with your hands when you are presenting, here are a couple of fallback gestures you can turn to:

- **Using Your Full Hand** - Pointing with your fingers at the slides or the audience is a less than desirable gesture. However, it is surprising just how many speakers make the mistake of inadvertently pointing to their presentation slides with their middle finger (yikes!) Pointing is never a recipe for success, especially if you are presenting in a foreign country where the gestures may signal something else. The worst thing you could do as a speaker is to give off a rude gesture and not even realize it. If you do need to point, the safest thing would be to use your whole hand instead.
- **No Fingers Near the Face** - The use of fingers can sometimes have unintended negative consequences. If you keep running your fingers through your hair, using it to push your glasses up repeatedly, scratch or rub your nose, or really touch any part of your face or body repeatedly, your audience is not going to be concentrating on what you are saying. They're going to be focused instead on your physical appearance. They'll automatically stop listening to you and start getting curious about why you are repeatedly doing this—which is why it is important to practice your speech several times before you give it, recording it if possible. You may have bad mannerisms or habits that you are not even aware of! Should you observe any of these mannerisms, make a note of this and assign specific hand gestures to accompany parts of your speech. This way, your fingers do not have the freedom to do as they please.
- **Avoid Your Fingernails** - Treat your fingernails as a taboo area during your speech. Don't touch them, do not play with them, do not even think about them at all if you can help it. A nervous tick that many speakers tend to be guilty of is playing or picking at their fingernails when they are speaking. To you, it may not mean anything because you do

not realize what you are doing. But to your audience who's watching your every move, it means something else entirely. Picking at your fingernails gives the impression that you are bored, your mind is somewhere else, and you are not fully present in the moment. Just like the finger rule above, when you aren't sure what to do with your hands, assign specific, strong hand gestures to each portion of your presentation, practicing until you get it right. You need to do something with your hands to keep them from doing the wrong thing. Read the portions of your speech that do not have any specific gestures at the moment, making note of which gestures you believe would be most beneficial to include in your speech.

- **No Wedding Ring Fiddling** - Nervous speakers are guilty of this if they wear a wedding ring. This often happens during the "awkward" phase of the presentation, when the talk is over, and you are standing there on the stage - sometimes in silence - as you wait for the audience to ask any questions they might have. As they glance out at their audience to see who has questions, these speakers will subconsciously be twisting or playing with their wedding rings. This speaks volumes to your audience. Either the speaker is nervous, or the speaker is impatient, ready to exit and call it a day! The wedding-ring-twist does not look professional, and even if you have done everything right up to that point, your entire presentation could be killed just by that one gesture alone. To keep yourself from doing this, steeple your fingers together as you patiently wait for some questions to come in.

- **Stay Away from the "Clinton Thumb"** - You'll notice a lot of politicians making this mistake. The Clinton Thumb involves your thumb resting on top of your fist. Doing this makes you look aggressive to your audience, especially if you pound the podium or the table when you do. Bill Clinton and John F. Kennedy may have done it, but that is not a good gesture to include in your public speaking sessions. It simply does not look natural. Choose to either steeple your hands together or drop them down to your sides for a minute or two (but not in a stiff manner) as you move on to your next point and prepare the next set of gestures for your speech. Keeping your hands by your sides is a quick reset button for when no hand gestures seem to feel right. Just remember not to leave them there for too long.

- **Stay Away from the Groin** - You would be surprised at just how many speakers make the mistake of clasping their hands in front of the groin area. That is absolutely the *wrong* move to make because it is only drawing your audience's attention to all the wrong places. This does not just apply to men either; women can be just as guilty of making this mistake. Clasping them in this way is not an effective use of your hand gestures and it may make you look awkward and uncomfortable. When in doubt, always use the hand steeple as your fallback move, and quickly move onto some other hand gesture for the rest of your speech.
- **Avoid Holding on to Objects** - Holding onto objects in your hand during your speech is risky because you might end up fiddling with them the entire time. Although experienced public speakers do hold pointers to help them transition from one slide to the next, they are conscious of what their hands are doing. You'll rarely ever see them fiddling with anything in their hands, as they do not want to distract their audience from the key message. If you do need to hold onto a pointer for your slides, be so subtle and discreet about it that your audience does not even know there is something in your hands.

Chapter 6: The Language of the Eyes

Pay close attention to the eyes; they may reveal that there is more to the story than what you are being told. When a person avoids eye contact, there is a strong possibility that they are uncomfortable, disinterested, nervous, bored, or all the above. If their pupils are dilated, it is safe to say that they are comfortable, perhaps they like you. If they are blinking far too much (in an unnatural way), there is a strong possibility that they may not be entirely honest with you. If they often look to the left, they could be recalling a genuine memory. If they often look to the right, it could be a sign that they are trying to make something up. Body language can be fascinating, almost like you are a detective trying to unravel the different layers of the story and get to the bottom of the truth.

Eye Contact and Public Speaking

As you can probably tell by now, there are a lot of factors contributing to your success as an effective public speaker, including your overall posture, breathing, the way that you carry yourself, the way you stand, and hand gestures. Another element to learn is *your eye contact*. If there was one thing you could do to enhance your presentation and the impact that you have as a speaker, it would be maintaining purposeful, deep eye contact with the members of your audience. Of course, it is impossible to do this with everyone, especially those seated all the way at the back of the room, too distant to see. However, for the audience members that you *can* connect wit - the ones seated in the first few rows at the front - that is what you should be doing.

There was an interesting experiment that researchers at Cornell University carried out. In a **study** published in the *Environment and Behavior* journal, the researchers took the cartoon rabbit on the Trix™ cereal boxes and manipulated its gaze. As a result of that one manipulation of the rabbit is eyes, adults were more likely to choose Trix™ over other cereal brands if the rabbit looked directly at them instead of looking away. Eye contact, as the researchers of this experiment discovered, invoked powerful emotions and feelings within the customer, and that sense of connection was what made them more likely to buy this cereal. Even a cartoon rabbit is eye contact makes a difference!

If you want to connect to your audience, you *must* look into their eyes as much as possible during your presentation. It's easier to do this when you are presenting in a meeting room full of colleagues at work; the room is likely smaller, with less listeners. In a larger venue, maintaining good eye contact with every audience member is a bit more challenging.

It's going to be to your advantage as a speaker, though, to lock eyes with your audience when you are addressing them, no matter the size of the crowd. Here's what good eye contact can do for you as a speaker:

- It allows you to appear more authoritative as a speaker, making you appear more believable in the eyes of your audience. Someone who knows what they are talking about will have no problems looking others in the eye and telling them the facts.

- It helps you concentrate on who you are targeting. Allowing your eyes to wander aimlessly could lead to distractions as you take in the external images or stimuli that are happening around the room.
- When you look them in the eye, your listener beings to focus on you instead of being distracted by their thoughts. It's hard not to pay attention when someone is looking you straight in the eye, and if you want to get your audience to focus, this is one way to do it.
- When your audience focuses on returning your eye contact, there is a greater chance that they are listening to what you are telling them. You are increasing the odds of your message resonating with your listeners.
- It helps to transform your audience from passive to active participants. When you look them in the eye, you are creating a connection, and it makes them feel as though you are speaking directly to them. Suddenly, your speech is no longer a speech, but a personal conversation which they are keen to participate in. Eye contact will help them keep up with your message.
- It gives you the opportunity to spot when your audience might need more convincing. When you make eye contact with them, you are simultaneously reading their facial expressions. When you see skepticism in their face, it gives you the chance to step in and convince them before moving onto your next point. Acknowledging their concerns by saying, *"I know it seems difficult to believe, but here's why it makes sense,"* will change the way that your speech is being received. Audiences will be intrigued when you appear to be able to answer their unspoken thoughts and convince them without them having to ask for more details. That's the power of good eye contact.
- It will force you to naturally slow down as you speak when you are looking someone in the eye anywhere from 3–5 seconds.

Former President Barack Obama employed this tactic to help him become a more powerful orator.
- It allows you to be both empathetic and assertive at the same time. You can share your opinion with your listeners, and at the same time observe their reaction, better understanding how they are responding to your message.

Good eye contact with your audience makes them feel like they matter. Despite being part of a large crowd, they get to feel involved in your presentation almost like it was tailor-made for them. In turn, you appear more approachable and a silent rapport is formed between you and the audience as you continue to engage them in your presentation with your eyes.

Strong Posture Makes a Difference

With the seemingly long list of things to do and remember for an effective presentation, it is easy to forget that your posture has to remain perfect through it all. If you are going to try and breathe the right way and give as much power to your vocals as possible, you are going to need good posture to support you through that effort. Proper posture does not just give the appearance of being someone who is confident and assured—it is also necessary to ensure that you are not breathing through your chest throughout your speech.

In Chapter 1, we discussed how being one with your breath is one of the most important techniques you need to master to become a masterful public speaker. Since the power of breath is so important, the subject is broached here once again, this time focusing on how it is linked to your posture. There's a lot of advice out there when it comes to public speaking, but the one piece to remember is: *breathing through your chest is never going to be good for your posture when you are presenting.*

Breathing through your chest is poor practice because:
- It facilitates a lot of tension in your upper body. When you are tense, it is going to negatively impact your posture, which eventually affects your public speaking capabilities.

- Chest breaths can't give you the same kind of sound quality that deep breathing can. When you are taking shorter breaths, you compromise your pitch, tone, volume, resonance, and overall sound quality of your voice. Only deep breathing promotes good posture.
- You're not fully utilizing your natural breathing mechanism when you breathe through your chest. By taking shorter breaths, you are not encouraging the use of your abdominal and diaphragm area, which are also an essential part of your breathing process.

When you are nervous, taking shorter and sharper breathes only makes it more apparent! You will appear panicked when your breathing is visibly quick and rapid, heaving and panting. Also, it is impossible to maintain good posture when you are not engaging your abdominal region. Think of your body as if it were a pipe. What happens when the pipe has bends or curves instead of being straight? It produces blockages. Those bends and blockages affect the flow of air through those pipes. It's the same thing with your body. If you were presenting behind a podium or a desk, any kind of bend forward or slump is going to make it hard for you to breathe properly; the quality of your voice *will be* compromised. The advice to hold your head up and stand up tall is not just for the benefit of the audience, but for *your breathing* benefit, too.

You probably understand by now: maintaining good posture is essential if you want your presentation to be considered a success. Not only does it make you appear confident, it also provides the following benefits:
- Taking deep breaths when your posture is correct helps feel calmer and more in control of your emotions.
- When you look authoritative, audiences tend to pay more attention to you compared to a speaker who looks visibly nervous, hunched, or appears as though they wish the ground would swallow them up!

- Good posture makes it easy for you to speak with clarity, so your words ring loud and clear across the entire room.
- It helps to create a better first impression among your audience. When you walk onto that stage with a strong, tall posture, the immediate first impression given is resoundingly positive. Now, imagine you were in the audience, watching a speaker enter the stage shuffling their feet, looking awkward with their shoulders rolled forward almost as if they were trying to retreat into themselves. Which speaker would leave a better impression in your mind?
- A strong posture conveys enthusiasm, and when you are excited about what you should say, your audience will sense that. Listeners are affected by your emotions – they can't help but feel what you feel.

Tips on Improving Your Posture

Ideally, you'd want to practice maintaining good posture every day and throughout the day, but that is not always possible. It's easy to forget about posture as you get caught up in your daily tasks. When you do remember, though, it is easy enough to work on improving your posture and to do it so subtly that no one even realizes you are doing it.

To improve your posture, straighten your back, imagining that there is a string at the top of your head that is pulling and lengthening your entire body upwards. When you are straightened as tall as you can, roll your shoulders back, tilt your chin forward slightly and lift your head up high. If there are people around you, try to imagine yourself attempting to peer over the tops of everyone's head. You should do this quick little exercise on the go or at home whenever you remember to be mindful of your posture. You should *especially* do it before your presentation. The more you exercise, the easier it will be to maintain good posture for longer periods until it eventually becomes second nature.

To help you maintain good posture, stand like this when facing a crowd:
- Your weight should be mostly on the balls of your feet, not on your toes, and evenly distributed across both feet.
- In order to avoid unnaturally standing ramrod straight, keep your knees slightly bent as you continue to lengthen through your spine.
- Stand with your feet no more than shoulder-width apart.
- As you stand tall and roll your shoulders back, tuck your stomach in for better balance.
- Keep your head level at all times. A good reminder is to check if your earlobes and your shoulders are in line. Your head should not be too far forward or too far back. Keep it in a nice, even line with your shoulder.

Tips to Improve Your Eye Contact

Instead of seeing your audience as a large group, start to think of them as one listener. From the moment you walk on stage and greet the crowd, start scanning the room and look around for friendly, warm, and welcoming faces. That's your first step to building a connection with them, shifting your gaze from one audience member to another as you hold each gaze for three to five seconds at a time. Once you have established that initial connection, these are some other things you can do to improve that visual connection with your listeners:
- **Focus on Everyone** - This one is much easier to do when you present to a smaller crowd, such as in a meeting room at your workplace. In a larger crowd, aim to connect with as many members of the audience as you can. An easy way to do this is to divide your audience into different segments or groups, and then choose several members of the group to make eye contact with.
- **Connect Just Long Enough to Make a *Connection*** - You do not have to hold their gaze for too long or make eye contact with only the same few audience members. That's going to

be impractical, as you are only allocated a certain period of time for your speech. What you need to aim for instead, is to make eye contact long enough for you to establish some sort of connection with them. During a presentation, each eye contact session should last no more than five seconds, which is the average time it takes to finish a train of thought. This way, you do not risk losing track of what you are saying, and the five-second rule encourages you to slow down the rate of your speech.
- **Avert When Sensing Discomfort** - Bear in mind that not everyone in your audience is going to be comfortable with direct eye contact. Some participants are shy individuals, preferring to blend into the crowd instead of feeling like they've been singled out. You need to be able to scan their emotions quickly when you are making eye contact—and as soon as you sense them feeling uncomfortable (shifting their eyes or fidgeting slightly in their seats), avert your gaze and move onto the next audience member. This is an important tip to keep in mind when you are presenting or speaking in a foreign country, as some cultures consider it offensive to make eye contact.
- **Connect During the Critical Parts** - There will be some points you wish to drill into the minds of listeners; time these key points so they match with eye contact you make. When it is time to emphasize a point, make sure you are holding the gaze of an audience member and look right at them as you get the point across. Your ability to combine eye contact with emotion will make your presentation much stronger.
- **Meet Your Audience Beforehand** – Whenever possible, try to meet at least a few audience members before you take the stage. When you walk in, you already have a few friendly faces to engage with! It can be difficult to make an immediate connection with total strangers, so it to introduce yourself to your audience beforehand, learning as few names as possible. Allowing listeners to get to know you personally

prior to your presentation makes they feel engaged when you connect with them again on that stage.

- **Watch for the Nod** - During your speech, one important audience reaction to watch for is "the nod." When your audience member feels like you have been talking to them and is feeling engaged and connected, they will subconsciously let you know by nodding along with what you are saying. When a person understands and processes what you have just said, they will nod to signal that, and you can take that as your cue that your message has been well received. It's also a great tip to pace yourself when you are speaking, by waiting for your audience to nod and signal that they've understood before moving on to your next point.

- **Avoid the "Lighthouse" Connection** - The "lighthouse" connection here is when a speaker moves around the room so quickly that it is impossible to make any real contact long enough to leave an impression. Like the light shining from a lighthouse, moving and scanning the ocean so quickly and systematically that it is already made a loop around and come back again before you can count to five. If you are scanning the room in this rapid, systematic manner, you are failing to make any real connections with your audience.

- **Don't Linger with Long Sentences** - You need to know when to move on, even if you are in the middle of a long sentence when you do. If you try maintaining eye contact with one audience member per sentence (exceeding the five-second), you run the risk of making that person feel uncomfortable. Your audience wants to feel connected, not *targeted*. If you do need to make the shift during a long sentence, make it subtle and gradually shift your gaze to the person sitting next to a time. Make it natural, not abrupt.

Quick Bonus Tip

When you are giving a speech across cultures, it helps to do some research, taking note of your listener's cultural norms. Showing sensitivity and respect for another culture's beliefs and perspective shows your empathy as a speaker, and your audience will look upon you favorably for demonstrating that kind of consideration.

In some Asian cultures, it is considered disrespectful to make eye contact, especially if you happen to be a subordinate. In Middle Eastern cultures, it is thought to be inappropriate for members of the opposite sex to make eye contact as it might denote romantic interests.

Chapter 7: Getting Over the Stage Fright Hump

What if you were told that even some of the best performers or public speakers out there had, at one time or another, experienced stage fright, too? Barbra Streisand, Meryl Streep, Elvis, Sir Laurence Olivier – all have admitted that they have had their fair share of stage fright jitters. It's perfectly normal to feel worried, anxious, and maybe even afraid at the thought of standing in front of a crowd and communicating in public. Not everyone was born with a natural love for the spotlight, and most exceptional public speakers today had to get over their own feelings of anxiety in terms of speaking in public. If they could overcome it, you certainly can, too.

More than 80% of the population experiences some form of anxiety or stage fright when asked to perform or present in public. Some might be reluctant to admit it, for fear of being perceived as weak, especially in a work environment where there is a lot of pressure to deliver exceptional performance for the sake of the job. However, denying the way that you feel is not going to help you in that department, either. Acknowledging your fears and gaining understanding of why you feel that way is the first step towards overcoming the stage fright hump once and for all.

Understanding What Stage Fright Is

Another term that is often used to refer to stage fright is *performance anxiety*. Typically, these emotions are experienced before you must make a public speech, perform or present for an audience. In some cases, stage fright can also be experienced when you know you must perform in front of a camera. Stage fright occurs in four stages:

- ***The Anticipation*** - Before the actual performance or public speaking session, the anticipation of what's to come can send your nerves into a tailspin. We tend to anticipate the worst, running all sorts of possible scenarios through our mind concerning what could go wrong on the day. These negative emotions contribute to the performance anxiety that we might be feeling.
- ***The Avoidance*** - Out of sheer nervousness, many might think about avoiding having to perform at all. Knowing there is no way out of the presentation can increase feelings of anxiety before the event.
- ***The Panic*** - This tends to occur right before you are expected to perform. It is not uncommon for many to experience sheer panic moments before taking the stage.
- ***The Appraisal*** - Performance anxiety can also take place *after* your big speech or performance. Some performers, upon reflection of how they think they did after the event, occasionally experience mild stage fright just recollecting the experience. This might put them off ever wanting to perform in public again.

Why Do We Experience Stage Fright?

There could be several reasons behind this, depending on your personality and past experiences. The most common reason is a lack of self-confidence. When speakers or performers do not believe in themselves enough, this leads to feelings of inadequacy.

Other possible reasons include a lack of preparation, fear of embarrassing or humiliating themselves in public; some performers even experience anxiety when they believe the audience is going to criticize them behind their backs.

Stage fright is physiological. When your body is faced with a stimulus, your immediate reaction can be either one of two things: feelings of excitement or feelings of fear. In the case of performing in public, it is often the latter that gets triggered, as very rarely does anyone feel immediate excitement when being told that they must perform in front of an audience. This stimulus triggers the adrenalin in your body—a hormone secreted to help you cope with the stimulus. Adrenalin, in turn, triggers the *fight or flight response*, which sometimes manifests into physical symptoms like shaking, difficulty breathing, rapid heartbeat, trembling, and even stomachache. These symptoms indicate that you are experiencing stage fright.

Are There Any Other Stage Fright Symptoms?

There could be several ways in which a person might respond to stage fright. This would depend on the level of anxiety they feel, as well as how badly they are affected by it. Stage fright symptoms are classified into two categories, emotional and physical.

Some of the common physical symptoms one might experience with stage fright include:
- Cold, shaking hands
- Rapid heartbeat
- Dry mouth
- Nausea
- Nervous mannerisms
- Visible trembling or shaking
- Weak in the knees
- Nausea
- Nervous flutters in the stomach
- Flushed or red face

Emotional symptoms associated with stage fright include:
- Feeling like your thoughts are racing all over the place

- Feelings of inadequacy or incompetence, which lead to emotional upset
- Anxiety about messing up what you need to say
- Fear of being embarrassed when you on the stage
- Feeling claustrophobic as if the room is closing in, struggling to remain calm or to breathe properly

In severe cases of stage fright, it is not uncommon for the speaker or performer to freeze on stage, unable to speak at all.

Is It Possible to Overcome Stage Fright?

Absolutely! With the right coping techniques, overcoming stage fright is entirely possible. The following measures are recommended for those seeking to deal with their nervous jitters and control their emotions before they take the stage:

- **Relaxation Exercises** - Meditation and yoga are among the recommended exercises to help cope with performance anxiety. Relaxation techniques are an effective way of alleviating the symptoms associated with the stress that the body feels when plagued by the emotional roller-coaster triggered by having to perform or present in public. If you need physical assistance to help alleviate your stress, *Shiatsu* massages (an Oriental massage technique) focuses on the pressure points of the body, working to relieve stress from those targeted areas.
- **Physical Exercises** - Relaxation exercises help to de-stress the mind, and physical exercises help you channel your anxious emotions externally in a healthy manner. Stage fright can cause a lot of negative, unhealthy emotions within you, and keeping them pent up is not an effective coping mechanism. You need to get the stress that you feel out of your body, and one approach to that is through physical exercise. For example, running, aerobics, kickboxing, hiking, and Zumba are exercises which not only help you work up a good sweat session, but they promote the release of endorphins in your body. Endorphins are brain chemicals that help you feel

happier and calmer—which is just what you need to deal with stage fright. There's also a quick little exercise that you can do right before you take the stage: rub your hands together as fast as you can, focusing on releasing all your anxiety through the motion. Another easy exercise is shaking your hands as fast as you can, putting all your energy into it at your fastest speed possible. Picture yourself shaking away the anxiety from your body.

- **Watching Your Diet** - The food you eat could be affecting your anxiety levels. If you are already feeling particularly nervous, avoid caffeinated beverages like tea and coffee right before your presentation. Caffeine is a known stimulant for jitters, and you certainly do not need the extra push; you are probably already nervous enough as it is! The best beverage to consume is water, making sure to stay well hydrated before and during your presentation to prevent the dry mouth sensation.

Understanding Speech Anxiety

Anxiety has a way of affecting our bodies in the most unpleasant way. No one likes feeling anxious, and we certainly do not want others to know just how jumbled our emotions are on the inside.

Not everyone is going to experience extreme stage fright, but most people will feel some level of speech anxiety when they must address a large group of people. Some people claim that public speaking is their greatest fear. Very rarely that you are going to find anyone who can confidently tell you they feel absolutely no fear at all when they have to present in front of an audience—so rare, in fact, that finding this one person is going to be like trying to find a needle in a haystack.

Don't be fooled by the calm, confident composure that you see many of today's renowned public speakers as they present. They are not completely worry-free;

they have simply learned how to control and handle their performance anxieties, turning that into a strength used to boost their performance. On the inside, they could be feeling just as nervous as you are! Although you may be trembling and shaking like a leaf on the inside, most of the time the sheer extent of your anxiety is not immediately visible to the audience. If you do a good job of covering it up, most people won't be able to tell that you are feeling nervous at all. Take comfort in the fact that your anxiety can remain hidden from the audience if you play your cards right.

Speech anxiety is not as bad as it may initially seem. The most anxious moments tend to happen *before* the speech, as you have no idea how is going to go; your mind may be whirling with all the possible ways which you might mess up. Once you take the stage and progress through your speech, you will likely begin feeling less anxious as you get closer to the end. Right before the speech, your anxiety levels might be at the highest point, but it gradually starts to fade away once your speech is in motion. By the time you reach the end, most people find their anxiety levels have dissipated, and they start to feel much better.

Anxiety is an all too common condition these days. In fact, anxiety has become the most **common form of mental illness**, affecting approximately 18% of adults. So, if you are worried that you are at a disadvantage because you seem to be coping with speech anxiety where others seem normal, do not be. Speech anxiety - along with other forms of anxiety-like phobias and generalized anxiety disorders - are more common than you think. When someone tells you that they have "butterflies" in their stomach or that they feel like they may vomit before a speech or presentation, that is form of speech anxiety. They may not be having a full-blown panic attack over it, but speech anxiety can manifest itself in minor ways, too.

Our bodies respond to fear in a powerful way. The most common symptoms experienced with speech anxiety are often racing hearts, shallow and rapid breathing, and cortisol – the hormone responsible for triggering those stressful emotions that we feel. Other general symptoms associated with speech anxiety might include sweating, light-headedness, upset stomach, possible nausea, and a shaky, unsteady voice. It may not be possible to eliminate anxiety over your public speaking moments completely, but there are a few ways you could deal with it to minimize the impact that speech anxiety has on your mind and body. Fortunately, these simple techniques will help you deal with speech anxiety and provide some much-needed relief when you need it most:

- *Technique #1 - Progressive Relaxation.* Best done while you are at home, lie down comfortably on your back. Keep your arms and your legs uncrossed as you do. Now, visualize a warm, comforting feeling that starts at the top of your head. This is where you imagine releasing all the tension that you feel from your body. After several deep breaths, imagine that warm sensation slowly traveling down towards the rest of your body. As you exhale each breath, feel the tension leaving your body. You should feel lighter and lighter and more relaxed with each breath that you take.
- *Technique #2 - Avoid Negative Self-Talk.* Avoid any kind of talk that is even bordering on negativity. In fact, avoid bleakness and cynicism all together! Whenever you notice your mind circling around a gloomy thought, put a stop to it, immediately shifting your thoughts to something positive that is ahead for you. It is extremely helpful to have several positive mantras or inspirational sayings on hand to help you turn your thoughts around and squash down the negative ones that threaten to aggravate your anxiety levels.
- *Technique #3 - Focus on Your Top Qualities.* This is an exercise you can work on before your presentation. Pick three things about yourself that you like and what you believe are your strengths. If you are struggling with this, enlist the help of a friend or family member to help you pinpoint some of your best qualities. Once you have picked three qualities that you like, repeat these qualities in your head, focusing on feeling good about yourself each time you do it. Repeated

this activity every day until you can mentally focus on these qualities – truly believing that you have them - and even with a smile on your face! This exercise helps reaffirm in your head and heart that you possess worthwhile and beneficial characteristics. Focus on your excellent attributes, feel the confidence, and believe that you are capable of handling this presentation.

- *Technique #4 - Identifying Your Triggers.* A big part of overcoming your speech anxiety includes being able to identify your triggers – getting to the root cause of what's making you feel so worried. Understanding the source of your fears will make it easier for you to break down those fears, allowing your mind to analyze and decide if there is a valid cause for concern. For example, once you have identified that your speech anxiety is stemming from the fear of what the audience might think about you, examine that trigger and identify if there is a *valid cause* for concern. Is there any evidence that you are going to be judged or criticized? Why do you believe your audience might think poorly of you? Have any past experiences given you a reason to believe that the audience might be judging you harshly? If they do think that way about you, are their thoughts going to impact your life in any significant way? As you slowly start to unravel the layers and find that your trigger is based on mostly assumptions, it is easier to keep yourself calm using logic and reason.

Don't forget about the deep breathing exercises and techniques that you learned in Chapter 1! In every exercise that you do to help you alleviate your anxieties over public speaking, always go back to *being one with your breath*. Deep, diaphragmatic breathing will get you through it.

Addressing the Negative Thoughts That Hold You Back

Anxiety and excessive worry are not feelings that should be taken lightly. Any kind of anxiety should be taken seriously; there have been instances where chronic worriers are so anxiety-ridden that they begin seeking out out harmful habits. Such habits (alcohol, drugs, smoking and even overeating) often represents an attempt to make themselves feel better, providing only temporary, short-term relief. These "answers" never work for long because they do not get to the root of the problem. Speech anxiety could border on these severe levels for some, and if you happen to be among those people who are deeply affected by this form of anxiety, do not dismiss it as something that is "just in your head."

In any area of your life where you hope to achieve success, there is one crucial element that must be present—*a positive attitude.* Unfortunately, it seems that more people today are plagued with negative emotions and thoughts more than ever before - possibly due to the very stressful lives most of us lead these days. The world may be a much easier place to live in, but it is also a complicated place. We have a lot more going on today than several decades ago, and the further we advance, the more reasons we seem to have to worry. We agonize about our lives, our future, our families, friends, job, kids - sometimes we even become overwrought about how to deal with those worries! Of course, we concern ourselves about giving speeches and embarrassing ourselves in public, too.

Negative thoughts prevent you from moving forward. When you are crippled by them, it becomes harder for you to focus on anything else, let alone progressing forward. Thus, is it imperative that you take the necessary steps to help you overcome these negative thoughts. They will only be a hindrance in your life *if you allow them to,* and this is what you need to do to put a stop to them once and for all:

- Stop comparing yourself to others—their story is not your story. You are living your own life, progressing at your own rate; trying to keep up with others when you are not ready is only going to leave you feeling frustrated and morally dejected.

- Stop overlooking your own accomplishments and start celebrating the victories you gain -even the little triumphs. Every step forward can server to reinforce your self-confidence, reminding you of the many things you are capable of. Treat yourself to a little self-praise!
- Stop second-guessing yourself—it will only cause you to spiral further down the negative slope. Be confident with the decisions you have made. Even if the outcomes seem like a mistake, be assured that there is a possible lesson to be learned from it, and that – in itself – is progress.
- Stop spending too much time with toxic individuals—they will only serve to feed into your negative thoughts and fears. Instead, surround yourself with like-minded people – those who have accomplished successes of their own, and those who inspire you to do better.
- Stop believing by default that everything is going to go badly. Unless you have proof that things are not going well, try working on the assumption that everything is going to perfectly. Turn that negative assumptions into positive beliefs!
- Stop judging yourself too harshly and learn to forgive yourself when you make mistakes. Mistakes are how we learn, and they are nothing to be ashamed of. They make us stronger, better, and wiser—which then leads to better decisions in the future.

Be Yourself. You are Good Enough

Putting a lot of expectations on ourselves to be someone that we're not only adds to the stress of speaking in public. You'd be surprised at just how much a big part of your public speaking worries comes from the pressure for perfection – a pressure that *you have placed on yourself.*

You *do not need* to be someone that you are not. You have plenty to offer by being yourself, and you do not have to pretend to be someone else. You do not have to be extremely charming, and you do not have to have the qualities of a movie star to be successful on stage. Being genuine and comfortable with who you are is often the best thing you can do for your performance, and when you embrace your own unique individuality, it takes a lot of pressure and weight off your shoulders.

Chapter 8: Push Without Being Pushy

Persuasion takes great skill. It's not easy to convince others to see things the way that you want them to. It's not impossible, but it takes a certain skill and ability to gently "push" them towards your point of view without being *pushy*. This technique is commonly referred to as *the art of persuasion*. You're *not forcing* them to go along with and accept the new ideas that you are presenting—you are simply channeling your communication skills *to persuade and convince* them to come around. Marketers and advertisers use this all the time—even salespeople sway customers into making a purchase from their business. Motivational speakers inspire change in others by persuading them to see the benefits of what great change can do for their lives. Steve Jobs, a man renowned for his ability to charm and persuade on stage, caused Apple's sales to soar after each presentation that he made.

Certainly, the art of persuasion is a valuable skill set to possess—but how do we learn to harness those powers of persuasion? Then, how do we then use those powers to our advantage during the speeches and presentations we give?

Persuading Your Audience in A Subtle Manner

The most effective speakers can convince their audiences and sway opinions without having to resort to being overly pushy, aggressive, or bulldozing their opinions unto others. Effective persuasion requires an entirely different approach. You need to take a step back and rely on empathy to understand where the other person might be coming from. Nobody likes being told they are wrong, and they especially do not like to feel as though they are being forced to change. They *definitely do not want* to have to sit through a presentation feeling as though ideas are being crammed down their throat against their will. Do that, and the only guaranteed outcome: you are going to lose your listener's attention, and their will to be attentive.

A subtler approach to persuasion is going to be far more effective. Arguing and debating the pros and cons with your audience will only take you so far. Demonstrating empathy, validating their emotions, *and then* working together with them to arrive at a happy and comfortable outcome: that is the very best way to persuade without being pushy.

The art of persuasion is called *an art* for a reason. It is not just about telling your audience what they should or shouldn't do. If you truly want to convince them through your presentation, you must make them believe in what you are telling them. They need to believe in it so much they are willing to take action; that is how the greatest speakers inspire change. You want your audience to leave your presentation with renewed motivation and eager to explore or further investigate the options you presented. You want them to leave your presentation, thinking, *"Wow! That was a fantastic speech!"*

To persuade without being pushy, you are going to have to be:
- **Trustworthy** - No one is going to be convinced by anything you say if they do not believe that they can trust you. You are a stranger to them in most cases, unless you are presenting to a room full of your colleagues or business

associates. When you are not known to your listeners, they are not likely to trust you the minute you step out onto that stage. You wouldn't trust someone you do not know, so why would they? But if you are honest and transparent and display all the right body language signals (open palms and good eye contact), as you progress throughout your speech, it becomes easier to convince them once they start getting comfortable. Once they see you are honest enough, they will be a lot more willing to consider changing their point of view. If you are in a situation where you are pressed for time to build trust (like when you are giving a speech), try building your case instead based on credible or reputable sources that are known to be trustworthy. Incorporate these reputable sources into your presentation as an added element of credibility.

- **Attuned to Their Needs** - What matters the most to your audience? Why are they here listening to your speech? If you want your message to resonate with your crowd, you need to speak to them where it touches them the most. Touch on the emotional element that was discussed previously. When you connect with them on the issues that matter most and what's important to them, you'll have a much easier time persuading them to see things from the angle you are presenting.
- **Confident Enough to Guarantee** - Only guarantee something if you are absolutely sure of what you are saying. If you believe that your recommendations are *the best and only* approach to go with, go out on a limb and reassure your audience by offering some kind of guarantee that would make them feel better about changing their mind. A "guarantee" might look something like this: *"Believe me, this works, and I'm living proof of that!"* Only do this if you are sure there is no way this could backfire, or you might risk hurting your credibility.
- **Honest About the Good and Bad** - It's easier to subtly sway your audience into seeing things from your perspective if you

are - once again - transparent about your arguments. Don't just talk about the positives in an attempt to persuade them. You need to present both sides of the story, the good and the bad, and then gently nudge them towards the side that you would like them to take. People are easier to convince when they believe that they arrived at the solution on their own. Use your gentle guidance to steer them in the right direction, and then let the final decision rest with them. Give them the opportunity to believe that arriving at a conclusion was due to their deductive reasoning; it was their idea all along!

- **Eager Without Sounding Desperate** - You may be eager to persuade them to change their minds but be careful not to let that eagerness show too much, or you might come across as desperate. Nothing pushes people away faster than desperation, and to avoid this, you need to take yourself out of the equation. Make your presentation all about *them, not you*.
- **Agreeable with Their Point of View** - During the Q&A portion of the presentation, you need to address and acknowledge their concerns, and even agree with their point of view as a display of empathy. Remember that no one likes to feel pressured into doing anything, and you'll have an easier time convincing them if you agree with their point of view every now and then. Show agreement by saying, *"I can see your point, and I agree that this is a cause for concern. However, I do believe..."* Validating their feelings tells them that how they feel matters to you, and that you are not merely trying to force your ideas upon them for your own benefit.

Finally, the most persuasive speakers always know when to step back. Trying to force anyone to agree with you immediately will do more harm than good. Take comfort in knowing that you have done your best, but at the end of the day, every audience member is a unique person with a mind of their own. They may be convinced – or they may not - but if you manage to pull off persuasion without being too forceful, most of your audience members should leave the room feeling agreeable with what you have just told them.

Using Body Language to Reinforce Your Points

Of all the public speaking techniques you have learned so far, your eye contact, tone of voice, and pauses during your speech are going to be the most helpful traits in this context. These skills, when performed correctly, will add more weight to your argument without you having to say the words out loud. Your body language is going to do much of the talking for you. The secret to successful persuasion is by focusing on *how or what you can do to be helpful to your audience*. That's what you need to aim for.

Most speakers, especially the new ones, tend to focus on how they can persuade their audience enough to get them to go along with their point of view. Instead, what they *really should* be focusing on is *how they can be helpful*. When you try to convince your audience from an angle that highlights the benefits of the solution that you are offering - addressing the needs of your listeners - it becomes much easier to get them to go along with your agenda.

People want to see what's in it for them, and when you can show them the ways they will benefit from your approach, they will be more than happy to hop over to your side without question. But do not forget you are not just trying to convince them with your words, you are trying to do it *with your body language*, too. Here's an interesting finding from a **University of British Columbia study (2013)** on the connection between eye contact and persuasion. The study found that in some situations, eye contact can produce significant help in situations where persuading another person is the goal. That said, keep in mind that in some circumstances, however, *too much* eye contact could cause your efforts to backfire. Instead of persuading your listener, you end up driving them away.

Eye contact has been mentioned several times already, and it makes another appearance here again because *it is so crucial* when you are communicating one-on-one or in a presentation to many people at one time. In short, effective personal communication cannot exist without the use of this essential process. You are going to have a hard time trying to persuade anybody if you can't even look them in the eye! Avoiding important eye contact may give them the impression that there is something fishy going on.

To be effectively persuasive, you are going to need to adjust the tone of your voice, too. When needed, you are going to have to change your vocal tone to effectively match the points and emphasis that you are trying to make. It's like tailoring the message to fit the audience you have in mind—except you are using your voice to do it. Your tone is going to depend on your context and the crowd that you are presenting to. If you are presenting to a group of colleagues at work, for example, then the tone you use should be professional and serious. Amongst general audience members, it can be jovial, upbeat, or a mixture of different emotions depending on the subject on which you are presenting. Avoid any language that sounds like it might carry an accusatory tone behind the message. Keep it neutral. Keep it professional. Most importantly, keep it to the point.

Another idea to keep at the forefront is that your audience may not always agree right away with what you are saying. Sometimes, they might not agree at all, and this might come up during the question and answer portion of your presentation. Your first instinct might be to get defensive, becoming immediately dismissive of their views, feeling the need to defend your views instead. That's not going to win you any points in the game of persuasion! You need to fight the natural tendency to jump to the defensive, taking a breath, using a pause, gathering your thoughts quickly before you respond. Remember to consider the tone of voice you are taking with your response. When you allow your audience to see that you are in control – even in situations sure to bring pressure to you – they will be impressed. This helps your listeners to warm up to your message even more (if they weren't already convinced before). Your tone takes precedence, in this case, as it can either win over your audience or cause an argumentative, heated debate; that is not how you want to end your presentation. Remember: eye contact, tone of voice, and pause. Use these together to create a winning, persuasive presentation.

The Importance of Knowing Your Audience

It will certainly help your persuasive efforts if you know and understand who you are talking to. Think of your presentation as if you are having a conversation with someone. The better you know the person, the more engaged, lively, and effective that conversational session is going to be. Knowing your audience works along the same principle lines. When you know who your audience is, it is easier to connect with them on an emotional level. This, in turn, makes it easier for you to persuade them because you have struck the right chord.

You *must* keep your audience in mind when preparing your presentation. If you do not understand your audience, how can they understand you? How will you convince to see why your presentation or speech can make a difference in their lives? Your goal is to show them that your solution is the answer that they have been searching for all along! Essentially, this is the goal of every successful communication: making yourself understood by others. You cannot expect listeners to understand you if you do not put them at the forefront of your mind as you prepare the content of your speech or presentation.

Think about the group of people you are speaking to. What kind of language would they respond to best? What types of words and vocabulary would they make the most connection with? What can you do to make your message resonate with them and make a lasting impression? Be sure only to use words that you are sure your audience is going to understand.

You wouldn't necessarily talk to your friends, family, co-workers, or acquaintances all in the same way. To be an effective and persuasive public speaker, you *must* be able to relate to the audience you are speaking to and make yourself more relatable to them, too.

For example, you wouldn't use the same acronyms, slang or jargon on a particular group when you know they are not going to understand or can relate to it. But you might use it on *another group* that you must present to because *they can* relate and appreciate the use of these elements. The best public speakers out there never use the same material repeatedly, even if they are giving multiple presentations. The most effective public speakers tailor their messages to their targeted audience, becoming familiar with that audience before they give their presentation.

The best way to find out if your message was communicated effectively enough is to ask your audience directly during the Q&A segment. Feedback can go a long way in helping you determine places you need improvement. Was your message clear and easy to understand? If you have not convinced your audience, the Question/Answer segment provides you with the opportunity find out why - and the chance to try again. This feedback is going to be crucial towards your other presentations moving forward if you must give the same speech to another group of people.

Using Humor to Put Your Audience at Ease

Humor does not just help lighten the mood and make your presentation more interesting; it helps to put your audience at ease, settling them into a relaxed, comfortable state, opening them up to persuasion. An audience member who is stiff, on edge and tense has a hard time being convinced by what you are saying. Mentally, they have already put up an invisible barrier, making them less receptive to ideas.

Humor can be a great tool when used correctly. Of course, there could be risks involved with this approach, such as when inappropriate jokes or references are used. This is just one more reason that your speech should be tailored to the audience that you are going to address; knowing who your audience is critical to keeping your humor in line with their humor! If humor is risky, you might be wondering if it is a good idea to go ahead and use it in your

presentations. The answer is yes—if you can, you should. Here's why the right kind of humor can be beneficial for your presentation:
- It relaxes both you and the audience. When the crowd is laughing along with you, it puts you at ease, alleviating some of the initial stress you might have felt at the start of the presentation.
- It makes you memorable. A public speaker who makes the audience laugh is one that is likely to be remembered instead of easily forgotten, as is the case with boring presenters.
- It bridges the gap between you and the audience. When you are laughing along with others, there is a sense of camaraderie that forms, and you feel almost as if you were friends. The ice is broken, and when everyone in the room is smiling, the atmosphere is visibly more relaxed.
- It captures your audiences' attention and keeps them interested. People are a lot more likely to listen closely to someone who is entertaining and funny.
- It makes you a much better speaker. Seeing your audience smile back at you will help you relax, allowing you to get comfortable enough to build a steady momentum when you are less worried.
- Public speaking can cause a great deal of anxiety for many speakers. But when you know that you have got what it takes to make your audience laugh, it can be a big help in easing some of that anxiety you feel. Hence, how do you use humor to your advantage and minimize the risks of it going south? You'll find these suggestions helpful:
- **Develop Your Own Anecdotes** - The best and most natural kind of humor stems from personal experiences. This kind of humor does not feel forced, which is good because then it does not seem like you are trying too hard. A possible low-risk option to play it safe would be to use a cartoon caption—if you can't think of any appropriate funny personal experiences to include.

- **Practice It on Others** - Before you present this delivery to a crowd, do a test run on a friend or family member, and observe their reaction. If they laugh the way you meant them to, then your audience is likely going to appreciate the joke, too.
- **Skip the Preview** - Humor should flow naturally as part of the conversation (or in this case, speech), so skip the preview and avoid the old, *"Here's a funny story" or "This is going to make you laugh."* Your audience can decide for themselves if your joke or story is funny enough. There's no need to announce that you are about to tell a funny joke or anecdote; it could backfire!
- **You Should Find It Funny** - Most importantly, you should find the joke or story funny, too. If you do not find it funny, it is likely your audience will not find it funny.

Chapter 9: You're Nearly There

A powerful speech comes down to the emotional value that it can offer the audience. It does not matter if your speech is 5-minutes, 20-minutes, or even an hour long. A 5-minute speech can be just as impactful as one that goes on for an hour if you know the essence of your message and deliver it effectively. When you find the essence, the crux, and the emotional value of your speech, that is when you can effectively gear your delivery and invoke an emotional response from your audience.

These are a few lessons that every public speaker should keep in mind to give powerful, emotional presentations every time:

- **Focus on the Problem Being Resolved** - This is a useful reminder when you are presenting on behalf of your company and trying to promote its products to your audience. A mistake made by a lot of speakers is to only focus on promotion, promotion, and promotion. While you may be doing what you are supposed to, this type of delivery puts audiences off. Focus instead on *showing them how to resolve the problems that they have.* Show them how the products are part of the puzzle, and how an effective solution you are offering can put those puzzle pieces together. Where

possible, use personal examples of your own experience they can relate to.
- **Your First Words Must Count** - First words often provide the initial impact and impression you make when meeting someone new. As the old adage goes: "You do not get a second chance to make a good first impression." This applies to the first time you meet someone, and likewise applies to your upcoming speaking premier. Your opening matters because it sets the tone for the rest of your speech. How memorable you are on stage is dependent upon the those first, carefully chosen words you say. To leave your mark on the audience, be sure to give some thoughtful consideration to your opening: what would be the most compelling story with which to begin? What might provoke a strong emotional reaction in your listeners, causing them to sit up and pay attention from the start? Will you be a surprising speaker, or a predictable presenter? Will you be going the extra miles to find that unexpected opener?
- **Speaking to Your Crowd** - The essence of your speech is not to merely stand up there and reading all the lines you are supposed to. To deliver that emotional value, you need to speak to your crowd the way you would with your friends or family – people who you genuinely care about. You need to appear unpretentious to your listeners, considering them as an important audience to reach, not just sets of ears to which you are churning out facts. Facts may be helpful, but stories and emotions are the elements that will keep them actively engaged, making your speech memorable.
- **Let Your Passion Shine Through** - Passion is everything in an emotional delivery, and you must be genuine about it. When you love something and believe in it with all your heart, that is going to show, giving your speech the powerful, emotional delivery that no amount of pretense or rehearsals could ever give. Passionate speakers are obvious. When you authentically care, it is written all over your body language

without you consciously remembering to watch that element of presentation. Passion must be the essence of your speech. Even the most mundane or dry topic can be utterly transformed if it is delivered by a passionate speaker.
- **Visualize Your Audience's Emotions** - To deliver a speech that really touches on your audiences' emotions, you need to *visualize the emotions you want them to feel.* What sort of emotions are you looking to invoke? What emotions do you want the essence of your speech to reflect? Once you have visualized the way you want your audience to feel, you can begin customizing your speech where each point that you make supports the emotions you are trying to invoke. Your audience may not be able to remember your exact speech word for word, but they will remember – for a long time – how your presentation made them *feel.* The best public speakers craft their presentations based on the emotions that they want their audience to feel at different segments of the speech.
- **Use "Grabbers"** - Want to make your audience feel at least one emotion or another throughout your speech? Use *grabbers* that pack an emotional punch right where they are going to feel it most. *Grabbers* are the few key phrases, statements, statistics, metaphors, or visuals that instantly "grab" the attention of your audience.
- **Make Your Content Emotional** - Don't focus on just delivering dry, mundane facts, and figures alone. You need to invoke the use of some thought-provoking, stirring sentiments in the phrases used throughout your speech. Emotions are going to be your most powerful weapon in any presentation. Yes, you need to deliver the facts, but instead of reading them to your audience, consider which phrases or key emotional words you can use to make the language more relatable to your crowd. If you want to make your audience feel something, you are going to have to use emotional words to back up your content.

- **Turning to Emotional Themes** - There are certain topics that have withstood the test of time and are still capable of invoking powerful emotional responses in your listener. Overcoming adversity, beating the odds, facing your fears, fighting for what's right, protecting the innocent, making a life-changing difference, heroic deeds; all are examples of emotional themes available for building your presentation. Look for ways you can naturally incorporate these themes into your speech.
- **Using an Emotional Tone** - You need to inject feeling and emotion into your voice and your tone, too, which is easy to do when you are passionate about your speech because it just comes naturally. It's easy to feel emotional when you are talking about a subject that you love. Your voice needs to reflect the emotional story that you are trying to tell. The right emotion and the right pauses during your speech can be powerful enough to bring tear to your audience's eyes. At the very least, look for stories that are appropriate to your subject and that will feelings deep within listeners.
- **Wrap It Up with A Punch** - Your conclusion needs to be just as powerful as your introduction was. Start with a bang and finish it with a bang. When you leave them with an emotional ending, your audience is going to say, *"Wow, that was incredible"* instead of thinking, *"I am SO glad that speech is finally over!"*
- More tips to keep your presentations as polished as possible include:
- **Don't Overdo the Words on Your Slide** – Many speeches include PowerPoint slides, giving your audience a point of reference. A common mistake made when using visual aids is making them too wordy. Your slides should only have the bare minimum text, choosing your words and visuals carefully. Are these the best possible representation of the essence of your speech? Condense and be concise. You do

not need a lot of words on your slides – you just need *the right* words.
- **Act Natural Through Mistakes** - If you happen to make a mistake or two during your speech, act natural, keeping the smooth flow of your words; it's likely your audience will not notice! Mistakes are only obvious if *you make them obvious*. Don't be nervous, and do not let it little errors mess with your mind. Mistakes happen, that is okay. Just play it cool and keep moving forward. No one needs to know unless you want them to.
- **Cut It in Half** - Think about how much time you have been allocated to speak. Then, think about everything that you want to say and how much you think you can fit into the allocated time slot you have been given. Got it? Now, take all that content and reduce it by half. Do not be the type of speaker who tells their crowd they are running out of time, and even though there is a lot more they would like to say, they can't. Keeping your focus narrow and concisely delivering your message is key to a polished, professional speech. Your aim is to whittle your content in half so that you have time to spare, having a few other topics on hand to discuss - just in case. If you find that you have more time than you expected, consider bringing up the "back-up" topics. Keep in mind, though, that many audiences find themselves thrilled at the prospect of ending a little earlier than anticipated. Ending early is much better than having to announce that you have run out of time with plenty more to say! That scenario makes your presentation seem incomplete, and your audience may be unhappy without experiencing the closure they were expecting.

Bonus Tip: The Best Way to Begin Your Speech

Can't think of ideas on how to begin your speech? Try the following suggestions as an effective "hook" to reel in your audience. Start with:

- A question
- A statistic
- An emotionally shocking statement
- A quote
- A testimony
- A personal anecdote
- A story
- A visual
- Some natural humor
- Some sound effects
- A physical demonstration using an object

Putting It All Together

Everything that has been discussed so far -*the power of breath, pause, pace, eye contact, posture, gestures, tone, and pitch* - are elements, when combined, that will transform you into an outstanding public speaker. You will find yourself capable of persuasion, evoking emotion, as well as engaging and convincing your audience. This will happen even if you are nervous about it and even if you struggle with stage fright. It is inevitable that at some point during our lives, we will all be required to speak in public. It could be a presentation in college, at work, speaking in front of a crowd representing the company you work for, or even having to give a speech as an expert in your field. Public speaking skills are a necessity, and instead of expending energy trying to avoid it, why not channel that energy into brushing up on your skills instead?

It seems like there is so much to think about and remember, and that can feel a little overwhelming. But remember that you do not have to do everything all at once. It's okay to take it one step and a time and learn to master one skill before you move on to the next. Becoming a public speaker that is the envy of others is going to take time (and countless practice sessions), so do not be discouraged about having to go slow. It's better to go slow and do it right from the beginning than to try and do it all at once and stumble along the way.

Patience and hard work will go a long way. Oh yes, it is going to take *a lot of hard work.* Here's a recap of how to put it all together:
- **Start with the Eyes** - Eye contact is your best relationship-building tool up while on the stage. Use it to your advantage. Audiences respond to a speaker who is connecting with them through the eyes, and you present yourself as someone who is trustworthy and honest when you can sustain good eye contact throughout your presentation. Don't forget to move your gaze around the room in a steady, controlled manner so that you are not just focusing on one person alone. Your aim is to connect with as many people as possible. Eye contact should be anywhere from three to five seconds per person, or as long as it takes for you to finish one thought. If the thought is long, break it up by shifting your gaze to the next person. Avoid sustaining eye contact; this can make your listeners uncomfortable.
- **Hand Gestures Are Helpful** – (Not to mention effective.) Combine them with the rest of your body language and put it all together to emphasize your strongest points in the speech. Use your gestures for emphasis, but do not overdo to the point of distraction, making it difficult for your audience to focus. If you do not know what to do with your hands at times, the best rule of them is to steeple your fingers together until you arrive at your next point and your next set of gestures. Avoid putting anything in your pockets or holding on to any physical objects to minimize the risk of fiddling. If you do need to hold onto a pointer for your slides, do it so discreetly that your audience is barely aware of it. Never fiddle, this gives the impression of nervousness and impatience. Keep your palms open and facing the audience, so you present yourself as someone trustworthy with nothing to hide.
- **Perfect Posture** - Your posture represents confidence, so make tall, strong posture a part of your overall body language. Stand straight like you are trying to lengthen your spine as

far as you can, and roll your shoulders back for the perfect, natural-looking confident posture. Avoid pacing on stage—this signals that you are nervous. Instead, aim for confident, well-timed strides at different intervals during your speech. If you must stand behind a podium or table, avoid leaning into these structures for support; doing so affects your ability to breathe deeply. If there is an option to avoid the podium, take it!

- **Emotional Facial Expressions** - Another body language element not to be overlooked is your facial expressions. Don't be afraid to use them to convey emotions, especially if you are trying to get your audience to feel just as emotional as you do. Keeping your expression strict and stony in a false attempt at professionalism will only backfire, making you seem aloof instead of relatable. If you are not conveying a range of emotions through your words and facial expression on stage, do not expect your audience to feel any kind of emotional connection to your speech either.

- **Remember to Vary Your Vocal Tone and Pace Yourself** - The *way you say it* matters just as much as what you say. You could be saying all the right things, but if your tone of voice falls flat and sounds uninspiring, it is not going to make much of a difference to your audience. Your tone is yet another tool that proves useful in striking an emotional response within your audience. If you want your audience to feel excited, your tone of voice should match the excitement *you feel*, the excitement *you want them to feel*. During the moments in your speech, which may be sad, let your tone of voice tell the story so that your audience feels just as emotional as you do. Simultaneously, your pace should be well-controlled throughout your entire presentation. Monospeaking and monotone pace are not going to do you any favors in your quest to become a more effective public speaker. Speaking too fast puts you at risk of swallowing your words, and the last thing you want is to see your

audience looking confused wondering what you just said! They will be too polite to interrupt, asking you to repeat or clarify the point.
- **Time Your Pauses** - Give your audience a chance to absorb your message fully with well-timed pauses throughout your presentation. Not only do you need to pace yourself, but you also need to know *when* you should stop speaking for several seconds. Public speaking is not a race, and if you have truly prepared and practiced, there is no reason to rush. You should prepare your presentation with ample time to deliver all that you need to - with time to spare. If you rush from one point to the next with no pause in between, it is going to be hard for your audience to keep up. Before they've even had time to digest the first bit of information you gave them, you are already rushing off to the next point. Pace yourself and pause, giving your audience the time necessary to process each point.
- **Key Takeaway Points**
- You must believe in yourself before others can believe in you as a speaker.
- Being a great speaker takes time and work, and it is going to take you several tries before you get it right.
- Never stop seeking feedback, even when you are great. There's always something that could use a little attention; there is always room for improvement.
- Appreciate all the constructive feedback you receive; the advice is meant to help you, not offend you!
- Build relationships with your audience before, during, and after your speech. Meet with them before your speech when possible. Communicate with your body language when you are on stage. Meet them after your presentation to seek feedback. The little things you do will go a long way towards making you a better speaker.

- Don't be afraid to show your audience your emotional side. They'll relate better to someone who's not afraid to make their passion than to a speaker who seems to be unapproachable.
- Make a genuine effort to connect with your audience. They'll respond well to sincerity.
- Making mistakes is not going to ruin your presentation completely. The way you handle yourself during and after those mistakes is the one that makes a difference.
- Forgive yourself if you make mistakes and take it as a lesson in stride. Even the best speakers out there have made some mistakes, so do not let it affect your confidence and weigh negatively on your mind.
- Stress-relieving exercises are going to make you a much better presenter if you use them beforehand. Less mental stress equals better on-stage performance.
- Always analyze your speech during your practice sessions and ask yourself how you can make it more engaging. Audience engagement is crucial to the success of your presentation. You can't call your speech a success if your audience is zoning out, barely remembering a word you have said.
- Listen to your audience and the concerns they raise during the Q&A portion of your presentation. Empathize with them and help them resolve the issues they face.
- Use humor in your speech to put your audience at ease. This opens them up to persuasion.
- Maintain the right body language all throughout your speech. Always stand straight and use diaphragmatic breathing.
- Avoid standing behind podiums or tables, as these create physical barriers between you and your audience.
- Share personal stories during your speech where possible—it is easier to invoke emotional responses from the audience when your stories come from the heart.
- Practice, practice, and then: practice some more - even when you think you have nailed it already. Repeat your

performance in front of friend or family (or a mirror) until you know your content like the back of your hand, and until you have your pauses well-timed and your gestures on point.

Conclusion

Thank you for making it through to the end of this book! Let's hope it was informative and able to provide you with all the tools you need to achieve your goals—whatever they may be.

Hopefully, you feel better equipped to become the masterful public speaker you always hoped you could be. You *CAN* do this, even if you feel nervous and your heart is beating so fast like it might explode out of your chest! Public speaking is inevitable, so you might as well learn how to cope and equip yourself with the necessary skills you need to survive and thrive.

Public speaking is about more than just the words you say and the way that you are saying them. Giving a speech is an opportunity to build, foster, strengthen, and even explore new relationships that may lead to even greater opportunities. Public speaking only seems terrifying because we feel like we're going through it alone—but you are *not alone*. Your audience is there with you, and when you can connect with them, it creates a sense of belonging. Instead of thinking about it as having to present to a room full of strangers, talk to your audience as though you were talking to a friend.

The final rule to improving and mastering your public speaking abilities once and for all is to *let go of the past*. Think of this stage as your rebirth. You're about to become a whole new person, wiser, more emotionally intelligent, and someone who's going to eventually develop the confidence you need to stand in front of a crowd when you must. Let go of the past experiences you have had with public speaking, especially if they have been unpleasant. Like a snake, you are going to have to shed your old skin, leaving your past behind and embracing this new version of yourself. Leave your old worries at the door and move forward with everything you have learned today to become a better public speaker tomorrow.

www.ingramcontent.com/pod-product-compliance
Lightning Source LLC
Chambersburg PA
CBHW070049230426
43661CB00005B/821